The King's Singers

A SELF-PORTRAIT

Nigel Perrin, Alastair Hume, Bill Ives,
Anthony Holt, Simon Carrington and Brian Kay

Foreword by Steve Race

ROBSON BOOKS

Authors' Note

The amazing thing about this book is that it happened at all! Many people ask many questions about how we operate, what happens when we are not on stage, and what sort of people we really are. This volume tries to answer some of the questions, as well as looking back over our dozen years, and is mainly based on an extensive diary which Brian kept in great detail, and which he assembled into the form of a journal, mainly for his own amusement. We all read it, took bits out, inserted others, and then Kit Coppard very kindly helped to organize and edit it, for which we are most grateful. We would also like to thank our own families, who allowed us away from home enough to live a working life worth writing about, and to you all, for running out of ideas for Christmas and birthday presents in time to add this to your list! Do read the book first – you will enjoy the movie so much more if you do!

Acknowledgements

We would like to give special thanks to Gemma Levine for the portraits of the King's Singers on pp 9-11.

For permission to reproduce photographs, thanks are due to: Yorkshire Television (pp 43, 44); *Radio Times* (pp 34, 58, 62, 64); BBC (p 60); Antony Miles (p 22); Suzie E. Maeder (p 104); Mike Beazley (p 52); James Clevett (p 55).

The cartoon on p 6 appears by kind permission of Martin Salisbury/ Shelley Masters & Co.

For permission to reproduce music, thanks are due to the following music publishers: Josef Weinberger Ltd (pp 45, 124-5); Lawrence Wright Music Ltd (p 126); Northern Songs Ltd (p 127); Chandos Music Ltd (p 129); Universal Edition Ltd (p 130); Schott & Co Ltd (p 120-1).

FIRST PUBLISHED IN GREAT BRITAIN IN 1980 BY ROBSON BOOKS LTD., 28 POLAND STREET, LONDON W1V 3DB. COPYRIGHT © 1980 THE KING'S SINGERS

British Library Cataloguing in Publication Data

King's Singers
   The King's Singers.
   1. King's Singers
   784'.092'2   ML421.K/

   ISBN 0-86051-109-X

Printed in Hungary   Endpapers: King's College Chapel, Cambridge.

Contents

Foreword

The King's Singers may well be the most arresting thing that has happened in British music since Haydn's *Surprise Symphony*. Not to overstate the case, let's just say that their blend is uncanny, their musicianship impeccable, and – most important of all – the breadth of their repertoire is a significant step towards the 'one music' so devoutly to be hoped for.

People talk a lot, and rightly so, about the King's Singers' meticulous musicianship. Rather less is said about their brilliant stage presentation. This is founded on a clear realization on their part, right from the start, that no one in his right mind wants to look at a young man in a baggy suit, still less a stained T-shirt. So neatness has been the order of the day. Six impeccably presentable, smilingly self-deprecating, charming young chaps line up for our approval, just as they might previously have lined up for a complimentary word from their headmaster at Gordonstoun or their commanding officer at Sandhurst.

Some people have been known to find this ultra-perfection ever so slightly irritating. It has to be admitted: I too have occasionally wished that a King's Singer would just once in his life sing flat, drop an aitch, or walk on stage with his fly undone. And yet, as the hostess said to her prospective son-in-law, 'Perfect manners cost nothing, and I insist upon them when the servants are present.' We in the audience are the King's Singers' devoted servants, and for us they put on a faultless show. Quite right too.

But they have another quality which I haven't seen noted elsewhere. Ziegfeld, or someone in the same line of business, used to point out that a well chosen chorus line offers at least one girl for each kind of male taste: a dizzy blonde, a pert redhead, a colleen, a spitfire, a waif. Look along the leggy line and somewhere you'll find your kind of girl. Turning the sexes round, I have a suspicion that something of the sort applies to the King's Singers *vis-à-vis* their female followers. Six in a row, all of them lovely. But look closer. There is the one who needs mothering; there the almost too good-looking one; there the one who'd be such fun at a wedding; there the one who's so like the chap who jilted poor Freda. And, my dear, the *names*! Nigel, Alastair, Anthony, Simon, Brian: it's almost too good to be true, like a page from the *Débutantes' Gazette*. Yes, admittedly, there's a Bill. But that just goes to show how splendidly democratic the others are.

To all six of them, my thanks for more than a decade of fine music-making. They're terrific.

Nigel Perrin

Countertenor

Alastair Hume

Countertenor

Bill Ives
Tenor

Anthony Holt
Baritone

Simon Carrington

Baritone

Brian Kay

Bass

The Story

The 1966 King's Choral Scholars with Sir David Willcocks, paying their repects to the Founder, King Henry VI in the middle of the front court at King's!

Programme Note

On our travels to distant parts of the world the first question we are asked by interviewers is invariably 'How did the King's Singers start?' Our response is usually on the following lines:

'Same old question,' says one.

'Do you mind the same old answer?' enquires another.

'It's really quite simple,' explains a third.

'Well, yes and no' (a hint of discord).

'Put it this way...' begins a fifth.

'Hey, listen—we check in at Schiphol in twenty minutes...'

If this conversation lacks concreteness (let alone a good scriptwriter), it's because we have never given much thought to the question until now. And so, on the risky premise that people other than interviewers might like to know a little more about us, we have stitched together this journal of the group's beginnings and career to date, together with some biographical notes and a few words about our music. First, however, a word of explanation. Today's King's Singers are Nigel Perrin and Alastair Hume (countertenors), Bill Ives (tenor), Anthony Holt and Simon Carrington (baritones) and Brian Kay (bass). Of these, only Al, Simon, and Brian were in at the start in 1965. Nigel and Tony joined in 1969 and Bill in 1978—and, for all they know, amnesia may have been the mother of invention in parts of the journal dealing with the periods before their time. Nevertheless, to avoid strangling the narrative with parenthetical disclaimers on behalf of the last three members, the journal employs the collective 'we' from the start.

We have been struggling for years to create an even better image than the one captured by this photographer back in 1965. Several things are worth noting, not the least of which is the magnificent Great West Door of King's College chapel in the background. The amount of hair, the number of chins, the length of the trousers, the cut of the jackets, the variation in bow ties and shoes, the relaxed stance, and the overall feeling of an early awareness of show-biz glamour are among the items which make this memento a collector's item.

Prelude

Our founder-members, Al Hume, Simon Carrington and Brian Kay, had the good fortune to be appointed choral scholars at King's College, Cambridge. There could be no better preparation for a career in vocal music. But an ability to sing collegiate church music of surpassing beauty does not in itself enable a group of such singers to please an extraordinarily wide range of audiences all over the world, or to evolve an enormous repertoire that extends from madrigals to pop—or even to attract invitations to sing at the Royal Variety Performance. This and much else has been our happy fate so far.

Certainly Al, Simon and Brian never envisaged our present way of life when they first came up to Kings. Simon recalls that, some years previously, he had seen a now-notorious 'home movie' called *A Day in the Life of a Choral Scholar*. It pictured a régime consisting (if his memory serves) of reveille sharp at 10 a.m. followed by tutorials at the Copper Kettle – the legendary Cambridge coffee house – throughout the morning and most of the afternoon. Studies were then interrupted by choir practice and evensong, so that the scholar could fulfil his work-norm only by putting in three hours' overtime at the pub before crawling off to bed.

The reality fell a little short of such exemplary dissipation. True, the first few days at college engendered unique feelings of freedom and security: there was money in one's pocket, a roof over one's head, and beer in the Buttery. But life for the choral scholar is pretty full. Much of his day, of course, is dominated by music—not only choir practice and evensong, but also the odd (sometimes very odd) hours he spends alone 'warming up' his voice. Music, however, is only one side of the scholar's life at college: like every other undergraduate, he is reading various subjects for his degree (and, if you are Al, you are also spending a lot of time on the squash court).

Collegiate life engenders a powerful sense of group identity in the choral scholars, of whom there are only fourteen at a time at King's. It is encouraged by their having at that time their own special table in Hall and draws strength from their common commitment to a special kind of music.

This group sense extends, of course, to spare-time activities. At Cambridge there's a continuous round of functions at which informal groups of singers and other musicians are asked to perform—not only traditional occasions such as May balls, rags, and music society gatherings, but parties of all kinds. For vocal groups such occasions call not for the classics but for 'fun music', especially close-harmony singing. There is a vast and varied repertoire to call on. High on most people's list of sources is the *Yale Song Book*, a collection compiled by the Yale University Glee Club under the great Marshall Bartholomew. Then there are countless volumes of Victorian and Edwardian glees, whose sometimes pallid or mawkish lyrics are often rescued by wonderful tunes; and the host of part-songs, from Elizabethan madrigals to modern pieces. In complete contrast is the great American treasury of close-harmony arrangements—everything from the 'barbershop' movement to the work of groups such as the Mills Brothers, the Inkspots, the Hi-Los, the Four Freshmen and many others.

Thomas Tallis His Canon – the King's choir boat which included in its team Simon, Brian, Al, Martin and Alastair. We used to stand on the bank before each race and irreverently sing: 'Forth in thy name O Lord we ROW!' Our technique was poor and, in spite of our innate sense of rhythm, we remained at the bottom of the river, where we belonged!

All these sources have influenced the style of informal group singing at Cambridge, and Al, Simon, and Brian were among those who happily continued and extended the tradition. They were members of the Footlights Club, and performing at club 'smokers' offered them early lessons in the art of coping with difficult surroundings and exacting, if friendly, audiences.

In 1965 they and the other choral scholars decided to make a private recording of some of the most popular items in the fun repertoire. Only 100 pressings were to be made for distributing among friends, but with their eyes on future stardom they chose the blatantly commercial group name of Schola Cantorum Pro Musica Profana in Cantabridgiense (hereinafter referred to as SCPMPIC). John Fisher made the recording in the Hall of King's College—a happy and significant event: John, who is administrator of the Bath Festival, still records our now traditional January concert in London.

Confident that the album would prove to be a landmark in musical history, six of the fourteen scholars set out during the summer on a singing tour of their old schools. They were Martin Lane, Al, Neil Jenkins, Richard Salter, Simon and Brian. They regretfully abandoned the SCPMPIC title—it was feared that someone might

Brian, Simon, Alastair and a part of Al are included in this photo of the King's Choir in 1964. The first two choristers in the front row are the sons of Sir Charles Groves and Neville Marriner.

fall over it and break a leg—and toured as 'Six Choral Scholars from King's College'. Not a wildly exciting name, perhaps, but it served its purpose—viz., the guarantee of travelling expenses, beer money and free school meals. The itinerary was King's School, Canterbury; Marlborough College; Tonbridge School; Bryanston School; and the Guildhall, York. As a gesture towards professionalism the group wore a

The schools' tour of 1965.

Al, Brian, Simon and Richard Salter, dressed for action in the choristers' cricket match at King's in 1965. The back of the photo refers to Lord Chief Justice Hume, Tuf Boots Foundation Scholar Kay, Cars Carrington and Colonel Salter!

special outfit, of which six pairs of sensible black shoes were the most impressive item; the wardrobe included corduroy jackets of interestingly different colours and cut, bow-ties whose patterns were incompatible but daring, and trousers that matched in the sense that all were dark and all were baggy.

Within its own modest terms the tour was a success, in spite of the fact that Simon was poisoned by lunch at Oxford and was, therefore, constantly dashing from the stage during the concert at Marlborough. The concerts were well received and the Six (as they were calling themselves by now) were steadily improving musically and in stage presentation.

Meanwhile the SCPMPIC record bore significant fruit. Brian had given a copy to Neville Marriner, founder/conductor of the Academy of St. Martin-in-the-Fields. Neville was planning a·concert for the Hale Arts Trust, an organization run by David Booth Jones at his family's magnificent home, Hale Park, a few miles south of Salisbury. David heard the record and wrote to Brian suggesting that a splinter group from the SCPMPIC might care to perform with the Academy at the concert.

Might care? It was one of those offers that can't be refused. Simon and Richard would have musical commitments elsewhere on the day, but it was quickly arranged that the other four would be joined by Robin Doveton and David Van Asch (who were both to become members of the Scholars group). The date of the concert was to be 11 August 1966. The prospect was obviously exciting, but something of the group's cheerfully amateurish approach to the affair is evident in Brian's account of how he spent the day before the evening at Hale Park:

'Although, of course, I was delighted at the idea of earning a few bob and meeting the members of the Academy again (they had made recordings with King's College Choir), I had more mundane matters to attend to. I had completed my last term at King's and was going up to Oxford to take the course for a Diploma in Education. It seemed sensible to drive from York, where I was staying with my parents, collect my belongings at Cambridge, and dump them at Oxford before going on to Hale Park.

'I set off from York at five in the morning in my 18-year-old Morris Eight. Before long it began to pour with rain. As always, this infuriated the car, which leapt off the road and attacked a tree, but luckily sustained only trivial contusions of the front wing. I reached Cambridge in time for breakfast at the Copper Kettle, collected my gear from King's, sped to Oxford, and after lunch set out for Hale Park. A slightly harassed David Booth Jones greeted my arrival with relief and gave me tea. There was much to be done before the concert, including a full-scale rehearsal, and I promised myself never again to allow anything but music to distract me on the day of a performance.'

The concert was to be performed under the portico at the front of the house, with the audience seated in rows of chairs on the great lawn. Well, of course, it rained; not a refreshing little summer shower, moreover, but a monsoon! So audience and performers squelched their way over to the church at Hale village nearby and the concert began a little behind schedule. All agreed that it was a success, and the members of the Academy were full of compliments and encouragement for the singers.

Earlier that year, what was basically the Schola Cantorum group— temporarily called the Scholars—made an album called *Songs of Love*. We recorded it not in a professional studio but in the Baptist Church in Cambridge (many of the tracks include the clearly audible twitterings of birds in the trees outside the hall). The album was commercially distributed—and it gave us our first experience of the legal minefields lurking in the recording business. The distributing company suggested to us that a contract would be unnecessary and we, green fellows, went along with them. Some years later, when the record was still being advertised in *The Gramophone* as one of the company's best-selling albums but we had had not a sniff of a royalty, it occurred to us that we had drawn the short straw. After an extended court case we were awarded the princely sum of £66—not quite enough to pay for the lavish holidays in the Bahamas that we had planned in anticipation.

Some months later David Booth Jones, by now a staunch ally, began to think of excuses for getting us together again. A good starting point seemed to be the appeals that were being launched jointly by the cathedrals of Winchester and Salisbury,

Hale Park

various concerts being among the money-raising activities that were planned. A convenient moment to discuss things came during the Festival of Church Music, which takes place every August in the lovely priory church of Edington, in Wiltshire. Several of us were among the group of choral scholars from King's who were to form part of the festival choir, and David invited us over to his house to rough out a programme. He warned us that, as Hale Park was at that time open to the public, all he could provide us with would be 'a snack in the stables'. David's idea of a snack consisted of such paltry fare as salmon pate, apricot syllabub, and other viands, which he forced down our throats with the help of surpassingly excellent wines. We were joined in the stables by Simon Preston (later to become organist at Christ Church, Oxford), who was in charge of the festival choir, and he at once agreed that a week of music at Hale Park was an attractive idea. The week was chosen and we hammered out the musical programme.

The whole affair turned out to be one of the happiest and most splendid that any of us could remember. Looking back on it now, we recall ruefully the amount of time that was available for long and relaxed rehearsals—something our crippling schedules deny us today. The concerts were well attended, thanks not least to David's excellent publicity machine. Apart from our delight in singing before appreciative audiences in beautiful surroundings, the concerts were notable for Simon Preston's brilliant accounts of Elgar's organ sonata and Liszt's *Ad Nos*. A feature of our concert in the Drawing Room at Hale Park was the performance of David's mother's geriatric parrot, which echoed in perfect pitch the notes of our countertenors (its sense of harmony, however, was only fair). The week seemed to pass in a flash, partly because we invariably slept until noon.

The Group Evolves

I

While we were sleeping the mornings away at Hale Park, the indefatigable David was planning our next step. It was to be a momentous one—a concert at the Queen Elizabeth Hall in London, no less, at which we and Simon Preston would join forces with the Academy of St. Martin-in-the-Fields. For us, of course, it was that magical occasion, the London début, and it meant that we had to find a name for the group.

We had plenty of time to decide: the QEH concert was to be on 1 May 1968. Meanwhile, to keep things ticking over while each of us pursued his separate career, we agreed that it might be 'rather amusing' to cut a disc or two. So we went along to Argo Records to see Mike Bremner, a friendly contact since our days of recording with the King's College Choir. Even at this stage our repertoire covered a wide field of musical tastes and Mike suggested we use two names—the King's Singers for the more serious stuff and the King's Swingers for pop. We went away to consider it; and we decided that the King's Singers would do for a start.

We now had to begin thinking about our programme for the QEH concert. One of our happiest decisions was to commission a work for the combined forces of the Academy, Simon Preston, and ourselves. The choice of composer fell on Sebastian Forbes. He had been a contemporary of ours at King's, and he was also known to many of the Academy players (his father, Watson Forbes, was for long the viola player in the Aeolian String Quartet). Sebastian's piece was the *Second Sequence of Carols*, which at the QEH was performed under his baton. This was the only work in the programme, as originally planned, in which we and the orchestra were jointly

A
C O N C E R T
to be given
in THE METHODIST SCHOOLROOM,
UPPER POPPLETON,
on Monday August 9th, 1965, at 7.30 p.m.
by
CHORAL SCHOLARS OF
KING'S COLLEGE, CAMBRIDGE

Martin Lane ... ... Counter-Tenor
Alistair Hume ... ... Counter-Tenor
Alistair Thompson ... ... Tenor
Richard Salter ... ... Baritone
Simon Carrington ... ... Bass
Brian Kay ... ... Bass

ADMISSION BY PROGRAMME ... 2/6
In Aid of Trust Funds

THE HALE ARTS TRUST
presents
AN OPEN-AIR CONCERT
by
THE ACADEMY OF
ST. MARTIN-IN-THE-FIELDS
and
CHORAL SCHOLARS OF
KING'S COLLEGE, CAMBRIDGE
at HALE PARK   near FORDINGBRIDGE
on THURSDAY, AUGUST 11th at 7.30 p.m.

Programme includes:
Concerto Grosso Op. 6 No. 4   Handel
Symphony for Strings No. 10 in B minor   Mendelssohn
Sonata for Strings in C   Rossini
Madrigals   Glees   Spirituals   Close Harmony

RESERVED SEATS (un-numbered):-   PARTIES OF
15/-, 12/6, 8/6   12 OR OVER 5/6
TICKET MONEY REFUNDED IF CONCERT IS
CANCELLED DUE TO WEATHER

QUEEN ELIZABETH HALL
General Manager: John Denison, C.B.E.
Wednesday, 1st May, 1968 at 7.45 p.m.
THE HALE ARTS TRUST LTD.
presents
THE ACADEMY OF
ST. MARTIN-IN-THE-FIELDS
Directed by NEVILLE MARRINER

"An hour's music, played with precision, care, consummate musicianship, and with more
sense of style than all the chamber orchestras in Europe put together." "The Gramophone."
SIMON PRESTON, Organ   BARRY TUCKWELL, Horn
and
THE KING'S SINGERS
MARTIN LANE - Counter-tenor   RICHARD SALTER - Baritone
ALASTAIR HUME - Counter-tenor   SIMON CARRINGTON - Bass
ALASTAIR THOMPSON - Tenor   BRIAN KAY - Bass

TICKETS : 25/- 20/- 15/- 12/6 7/6
Areas   C   B   D   A   E
Booking from 1st April
From ROYAL FESTIVAL HALL BOX OFFICE, S.E.1 (01-928 3191) and usual Agents
Please enclose a stamped addressed envelope with postal applications. Programme overleaf . . .

THE HALE ARTS TRUST
presents
SIMON PRESTON
with past and present
CHORAL SCHOLARS OF KING'S COLLEGE
CAMBRIDGE
MARTIN LANE - Counter tenor
ALISTAIR HUME - Counter tenor   RICHARD SALTER - Baritone
ALASTAIR THOMPSON - Tenor   SIMON CARRINGTON - Bass
                                  BRIAN KAY - Bass
In a Recital for Organ and Voices
on FRIDAY, 1st SEPTEMBER, 1967 at 8 p.m.
in WINCHESTER CATHEDRAL
In aid of the Cathedral Appeal

The Programme includes : - FANTASIA IN C MINOR - J. S. BACH
FANTASIA & FUGUE ON THE CHORALE
"Ad nos ad salutarem undam" - LISZT
THE ORGAN SONATA IN G MAJOR (1st movement) - ELGAR
MOTETS, ANTHEMS and SPIRITUALS from the 15th to 20th Century

"THE TIMES"
"The main enjoyment of the evening came from two of the qualities
that have already made Mr. Preston one of our leading organists, his
apparently complete mastery of any organ he lays hands on, and his
musicianly ability to use so versatile an instrument as this to its full
potential."
"DAILY MAIL"
"Simon Preston's brilliant recital on the Abbey organ confirms him
as the outstanding player of his generation."

Reserved Seats 20/-, 15/- (numbered)
10/-, 5/-
from Whitwam's, 70 High Street,
Winchester   Tel. 5253
and at the door of the Cathedral from
7 p.m.
Light refreshments will be on sale
during the Interval

involved. However, we had devised a set of pop-song arrangements to conclude our part in the concert, and we were kind enough to suggest that, if the Academy had ever aspired to the status of a backing group, now was the moment to seize their chance. For a moment they were dumbfounded; but they decided to take the plunge—and the set went with a swing.

In fact the whole concert seemed to go so marvellously well that none of us wanted it to end. It was followed by a champagne party in the foyer, a late dinner at a Kensington hotel, and then a get-together at the flat next door to Westminster Cathedral that Brian and Martin Lane shared at the time. We sat up most of the night talking excitedly, drinking a lot, and waiting in fear and trembling for the early editions of the newspapers. Eventually the suspense proved insupportable and several of us drove down to Fleet Street to snatch the papers hot from the presses. The reviews were distinctly encouraging ('singers of resource'—*The Times*), and we were elated.

We savoured the moment for what it was—a delightful, but quite isolated, experience: at the time, and for most of the next year or so, we rarely had any firm conviction that we had prepared the ground for a career. As it turned out, we made six public appearances during the six months after the QEH concert. We were invited to the Cambridge festival, where our light-hearted concert at Sidney Sussex College was notable for the first (and last) public performance of a disgracefully camp version by Al and Martin of *You're a Lady*, a contemporary hit of Abi and Esther Ofarim. For two concerts, in Hereford and at Eton College, both in September, we were joined by the jazz bass-player Peter Ind. When, on one occasion, we had the temerity to cast doubt on Peter's sense of rhythm, he put us firmly in our place by remarking that the great Coleman Hawkins had found it adequate to his needs.

The Eton concert proved to be the last with the original six members of the group. During the concert it became apparent that Martin was out of sorts and had difficulty in concentrating his attention. A few days later he told Brian that he had twice found himself almost walking under a bus on his way home from work. On his doctor's advice he was examined by a brain specialist, who quickly located a tumour. This was a crushing blow: Martin had a magnificent voice and he was a close friend of us all—especially of Simon's, the two having been choristers at Christ Church, Oxford, and contemporaries at King's School, Canterbury, before their Cambridge days. Thankfully, Martin was to make a remarkable recovery, but he was no longer able to sing with us.

Martin's illness was the only occasion in our career when we have had to cancel a concert. But there were more bookings in our diary, so we had to make a quick decision about what to do. It was not, of course, nearly so difficult a problem as it would have been a year or two later. Our work as a group was still very much a spare-time activity, each of us having a musical or other job to keep the bailiff from the door. Moreover, although we were beginning to evolve a concert formula, our ideas were still undeveloped and our style and repertoire were not so very different from several other groups of singers who were around at the time.

There did not seem to be any suitable countertenors available: we all knew Nigel Perrin by then, but he would not be leaving King's until the following summer. So we went to see an old friend, Felicity Palmer, and asked her to be our top voice for a time. She agreed, and quickly settled in as a member of the team; and her soprano voice instantly expanded our possible repertoire. Bearing in mind how famous she has become, we recall a little wryly a BBC World Service recording we made in 1969, which included Felicity singing such noble arias as *In the Mood* and *You're Getting to be a Habit with Me*.

And so into 1969—and, almost immediately, another blow. Richard Salter, our first baritone, had the misfortune – from our point of view – to be awarded one of the prestigious Richard Tauber Scholarships, which meant that he would be departing for Vienna almost at once. Tony Holt was teaching and making music in Chichester at that time and couldn't be budged, so we asked Nigel Beavan (later to be appointed to the choir of St. Paul's Cathedral) to oblige. In case this shuffling of personnel is beginning to resemble a three-card (or rather six-card) trick, here is the line-up for a concert we gave at Radley School, near Oxford in February 1969: Felicity Palmer (soprano), Al Hume (countertenor), Alastair Thompson (tenor), Nigel Beavan and Simon Carrington (baritones) and Brian Kay (bass). The programme that evening is fairly typical of our musical offerings at the time:

PART ONE (in the Chapel)

16th and 17th Centuries
Cantate Domino	Pitoni
Beata es	Jacob Handl
Laetentur coeli	Hassler
O Lord, give Thy Holy Spirit	Tallis
Alleluia	Weelkes

Organ Music

20th Century
O bone Jesu	Philip Radcliffe
Lullaby	Christopher Brown
O sacrum convivium	Messiaen
There is no rose	Simon Preston

Organ Music

Spirituals
By and by	arr. Ken Naylor
Peter go ring dem bells	arr. Ken Naylor
Joshua fit de battle	arr. Robert Sells

PART TWO (in School)

O lusty May	anon. 15th cent.
I love, alas, I love thee	Thomas Morley
Foresters, sound the cheerful horn	Sir Henry Bishop
I gave my love a cherry	Paddy Roberts
Early one morning	trad. arr. Sebastian Forbes
Wives and lovers	Bacharach arr. Christopher Bowers-Broadbent
Silvery moon	arr. Robin Nelson
Animals	arr. Marshall Bartholomew
My ship	Kurt Weill
You're getting to be a habit	arr. Johnnie Walker
The mermaid	arr. John Whitworth

One of our most interesting projects that year was to research and record the music for the York Mystery Plays, that wonderful cycle of fourteenth-century vernacular religious drama. Simon has always had the privilege of (Simon: 'been lumbered with') finding additions to our repertoire, so he set about looking for musical items that were from the right period, were apt for the particular moments in the drama for which they were required, and were suitable for our singing resources—a fairly hair-raising task. Felicity could not be with us on this occasion, so we enlisted the aid of James Bowman, a friend of Simon and Brian's from their Oxford days and, incidentally, a contemporary of Tony's at university and already regarded as one of the finest countertenors in Britain. The York Festival that year also included a concert by Simon Preston and ourselves in the chapel of St. John's College. Although enjoyable in many ways, the week in York was hardly an ideal exposure for us: the Mystery Plays music did not involve an actual appearance, and someone forgot to print programmes for the concert.

II

Better days were just around the corner: the beginning of our long relationship with the BBC. It started with the Home Service (Radio Four's ancestor) and, specifically, two programmes that helped to make the King's Singers a name well known all over the country. The first was *Morning Melody*, produced at that time by Bill Relton, who was later to become manager of the BBC Symphony Orchestra. The second was Steve Race's *Invitation to Music*, to which we first contributed a year later (as will be seen). The man in charge of contracts at the BBC was Peter Marchbank, another friend from our student days. We have no proof, but we entertain a powerful suspicion, that Peter was responsible for our first BBC cheque being made in favour of 'The King's Sisters'.

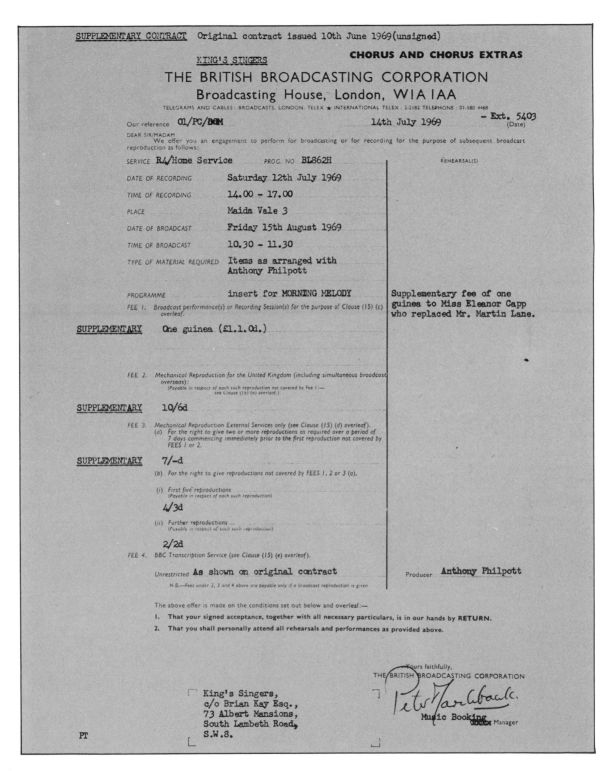

SUPPLEMENTARY CONTRACT   Original contract issued 10th June 1969(unsigned)

KING'S SINGERS   **CHORUS AND CHORUS EXTRAS**

THE BRITISH BROADCASTING CORPORATION
Broadcasting House, London, W1A 1AA
TELEGRAMS AND CABLES : BROADCASTS. LONDON. TELEX ★ INTERNATIONAL TELEX : 2-2182 TELEPHONE : 01-580 4468

Our reference   01/PC/BGM   14th July 1969   — Ext. 5403
                                                                (Date)
DEAR SIR/MADAM
          We offer you an engagement to perform for broadcasting or for recording for the purpose of subsequent broadcast
reproduction as follows:

SERVICE R4/Home Service   PROG. NO BL862H   REHEARSAL(S)

DATE OF RECORDING   Saturday 12th July 1969

TIME OF RECORDING   14.00 - 17.00

PLACE   Maida Vale 3

DATE OF BROADCAST   Friday 15th August 1969

TIME OF BROADCAST   10.30 - 11.30

TYPE OF MATERIAL REQUIRED   Items as arranged with
                            Anthony Philpott

PROGRAMME   insert for MORNING MELODY   Supplementary fee of one
                                                           guinea to Miss Eleanor Capp
FEE 1. Broadcast performance(s) or Recording Session(s) for the purpose of Clause (15) (c)   who replaced Mr. Martin Lane.
        overleaf.

SUPPLEMENTARY   One guinea (£1.1.0d.)

FEE 2. Mechanical Reproduction for the United Kingdom (including simultaneous broadcast
        overseas):
            (Payable in respect of each such reproduction not covered by Fee 1:—
                    see Clause (15) (a) overleaf.)

SUPPLEMENTARY   10/6d

FEE 3. Mechanical Reproduction External Services only (see Clause (15) (d) overleaf).
        (a) For the right to give two or more reproductions as required over a period of
             7 days commencing immediately prior to the first reproduction not covered by
             FEES 1 or 2.

SUPPLEMENTARY   7/–d

        (b) For the right to give reproductions not covered by FEES 1, 2 or 3 (a).

        (i) First five reproductions
             (Payable in respect of each such reproduction)

             4/3d

        (ii) Further reproductions
              (Payable in respect of each such reproduction)

             2/2d

FEE 4. BBC Transcription Service (see Clause (15) (e) overleaf).

        Unrestricted As shown on original contract   Producer   Anthony Philpott

             N.B.—Fees under 2, 3 and 4 above are payable only if a broadcast reproduction is given

The above offer is made on the conditions set out below and overleaf:—

1.   That your signed acceptance, together with all necessary particulars, is in our hands by **RETURN**.

2.   That you shall personally attend all rehearsals and performances as provided above.

                                              Yours faithfully,
                                          THE BRITISH BROADCASTING CORPORATION

        King's Singers,
        c/o Brian Kay Esq.,
        73 Albert Mansions,
        South Lambeth Road,   Music Booking   Manager
        S.W.8.
PT

Early evidence of our breakthrough into the big money league.

Nigel Perrin graduated from Cambridge that summer and we all hoped that he would become the permanent replacement for Martin. Nigel certainly liked the idea, but there was a problem. He had already become a member of another group of ex-Kingsmen, the Scholars not to be confused with the SCPMPIC who used the name on the one occasion of the *Songs of Love* album. For the next few months the Scholars and the King's Singers competed in the race for super-stardom (well, the occasional friendly word in a provincial paper) with Nigel as top voice in both groups. Eventually he decided that this was too much of a good thing—and chose to stay with us. He was replaced in the Scholars by a soprano, so that in musical terms the two groups were no longer rivals. Nonetheless, we were both appearing at the same sort of venues during the next year or two—a period in which Alan Blyth, writing in the *Musical Times*, referred to us as 'the darling of the music clubs'!

Such clubs or societies certainly formed our principal outlet at that time. A long-remembered incident occurred at one of them, the society run for its staff by the John Lewis department store in Oxford Street, London. The location was the store's small concert hall, which was next door to the toy department. The hall has an elevated gallery running around all four sides and has its own access door. On this occasion the gallery walls were hung with paintings by members of the staff. Our concert began with a solemn, beautiful church motet by William Byrd. When it finished there was one of those pregnant silences that follow an especially lovely piece of music. Then the door of the gallery flew open, and a lady was heard to shout to an unseen companion: 'You go on, love—I'll just have a look at the nudes.' Down below, in the front row of the hall, were several of our friends. We looked at them. They looked at us. Then eyes were quickly averted to forestall an outburst of hysteria. Somehow we re-assembled our faculties, cleared our throats, and carried on: by then, the art patron had vanished. (We owe a good deal to John Lewis, by the way. Over the next few years we performed concerts in several places under their sponsorship; they contributed to the cost of our performing suits; and they commissioned new works for us.)

By the end of 1969, Tony had left Chichester and we had assembled, at last, the group that was to constitute the King's Singers until the spring of 1978: Nigel Perrin and Al Hume (countertenors), Alastair Thompson (tenor), Tony Holt and Simon Carrington (baritones) and Brian Kay (bass).

Invitations to Music

I

The first concert of the new team was at Stockport School in January 1970. It was at once a pleasurable occasion and a significant precedent—the first of a series of concerts at the school that were to be held each January for several consecutive years. They had a unique place in our calendar, because they were usually the last ones before what was to become our traditional January concert at the Queen Elizabeth Hall in London. Stockport gave us the chance, away from the professional critics, to try out in public the new programme we had evolved for the QEH. We like to think that, for every member of our Stockport audiences who might have objected to being treated as a guinea-pig, there were several others who relished the idea of being one step ahead of the metropolis.

The period from the start of 1970 to mid-1972 can be seen in retrospect as the watershed in our career. For much of this time, we continued to follow our individual careers (four of us in cathedral choirs, Al and Simon as double-bass players in symphony orchestras); on the other hand, the group was gradually becoming better known and was attracting bookings all over the place. In 1970 our most significant (and in many ways happiest) work was our involvement with the radio programme *Invitation to Music*. This was a marvellous shop-window for us: the programme went out every afternoon, and each week it featured a particular artist or group. Our appearances on it gave us a great opportunity to expand our repertoire and develop different styles of presentation. In both these aspects we were guided by the producer, Alan Owen, who was to become a close friend. Steve Race took a great interest in our style and sound, and his enthusiasm helped immeasurably in building for us a large following of radio listeners.

The period of our association with Steve's programme saw a marked increase in the size and range of our concert audiences. We seemed to have reached a stage when quite a number of fans were regularly attending all our major concerts all over the country: these, presumably, were the people a writer on the *Guardian* referred to as our 'middle-aged groupies'. Over the years, the average age of our audiences has dropped. We ignore cynics who assert this is merely an impression created by our own advancing years. At all events, our concert material and methods of presentation in 1970 were of a kind to appeal more to an older, or at least more classically inclined, generation.

One of the landmarks that year was a cabaret stint aboard the P & O liner *Chusan* on one of its cruises in the Mediterranean region. The ship was due to sail early in the morning, so we travelled down to Southampton the night before. Brian and Nigel booked into a hotel, and in a fit of prudence decided to economize by sharing a

Probably our earliest cabaret appearance – on board the P. and O. cruise ship *Chusan*, somewhere in the Mediterranean, in the summer of 1969.

double room. The following morning they were presented with a bill made out, with suggestive ambiguity, to 'Mr B. Kay and Friend'! At this time Nigel was already a happily married man, and Brian was to be wed immediately after the ship returned to port; but such things count for nothing in the mind of a congenitally suspicious dockside hotel manager.

The cruise was a valuable experience for us. The audiences were appreciative, and the general ambience turned our thoughts to possibilities in the cabaret field at home. Another important aspect was that in the ship's bars you could buy four Pimm's No.1 for 8/8d. We all displayed enviable *savoir faire* in our dealings with foreigners afloat and ashore. One thinks, for instance, of the splendidly imperious way in which Al dismissed a tiny beggar who had pursued him the length and breadth of Funchal (Madeira) demanding cash or similar negotiables: 'See here, my man, ten out of ten for perseverance; but you are obviously much better dressed than me, so buzz off!' And then, on board ship, it was wonderful to see how Tony managed to conceal his relief when, leaping to his feet after a beautiful German girl invited him to play with her, he discovered that all she wanted was a game of ping-pong.

A couple of days before the cruise we had recorded a demo-tape to present to a record company that had expressed interest in us. We had been introduced to Gordon Langford, who arranged for us a couple of songs, *Peanut Vendor* and *Time Was*. The tape eventually formed the basis of our *By Appointment* album. Gordon was to become our principal arranger for many years—his masterpieces include two of our most popular traditional numbers, *Widdecombe Fair* and *The Lass of Richmond Hill*—and he is still one of our favourite collaborators. Through Gordon's musical connections, which are legion, we met Ron Goodwin, who was asked to write a song about us for inclusion on the album. The result was a classic:

Oh what kind of things do the King's Singers sing
When we sing at a sing-song or that kind of thing?
We've part-songs and madrigals, sea shanties and pop,
With a doo-wap-doo-wap-doo-wap, doo-wap-doo-wap-doo-wap-bop.

We switch from the classics to songs of romance,
We sing in a church or we sing at a dance,
We'll sing the old masters, then just for a laugh
We'll swing into Bacharach and back again to Bach!

We've songs that are sonorous and onerous and gay,
And one by King Henry the Eighth, by the way;
There's Grieg and Vittoria and moria than that—
We'll sing you a glorious magnificat!

We sing Monteverdi, Vivaldi and Byrd,
And the way we sing Tallis has got to be heard
We vary the songs and we vary the pace,
With two altos, one tenor, two baritones, one bass.

(Al)
And when people ask how I sing in the bath
I look academic and try not to laugh:

(Brian)
A damn silly question, I do so agree,
I wonder why nobody thinks of asking me!

So these are the things that the King's Singers sing
When we sing at a party or that kind of thing.
We've skimmed from our repertoire a few off the top,
With a doo-wap-doo-wap-doo-wap-doo-wap, doo-wap-doo-wap-doo-wap-doo-wap,
Folk songs, church music, traditional and pop!

We did not complete the album until the following year, and it did not appear in the shops until 1972, but it proved its stamina: after doing well on the Enterprise label it was reissued by Polydor, and it has continued to sell to this day.

A beaming family group, with Gordon Langford (Peanut Vendor, Lass of Richmond Hill, Widdecombe Fair, etc.) at the piano.

II

On 1 October 1970 we had finished a concert at the Kensington Music Club when our dressing-room door was thrown open and in marched a complete stranger, who announced that he had just completed a musical work that, he had decided, was an ideal vehicle for the King's Singers. The fellow was very persistent, so we agreed to meet him later to talk things over. And so began our friendship with Joseph Horovitz, one of the most delightful and diversely talented composers it has been our pleasure to work with. The piece in question was *Captain Noah and His Floating Zoo*, which he had written with Michael Flanders. It was the centre-piece of our Queen Elizabeth Hall concert the following January, became a regular item in our collaborations with Jo's trio, was included on an LP, was broadcast and televised often and in general proved to be one of the best liked pieces of the early years of the group.

The last three months of the year were our busiest yet. In November our bottom half (Tony, Simon and Brian) took part in a concert in the Purcell Room (part of the South Bank complex) with David Munrow and his Early Music Consort. Their role was to 'enrich' one of David's always adventurous programmes with a selection of rounds and catches—not all of them lacking in salacity (perhaps this was what the *Daily Telegraph* critic was referring to when he wrote of the trio's 'disarming camaraderie').

David was another of our Cambridge contemporaries; Simon had played in several ensembles with him there, and we had since worked often with him. He collaborated with us on our *French Collection* album, which included several madrigals in which we were accompanied by the Consort. The last occasion on which we worked together before his shockingly untimely death was when he taped an interview with us for his delightful *Pied Piper* programme on Radio Three. David had a genius for many things, but manipulating tape recorders was not one of them. After fiddling with one of the BBC's very sophisticated Uher machines for several minutes, he finally got it to work; still a bit flustered after his electronic tinkering, he thrust the microphone under Nigel's nose and enquired, in his best interviewer's voice:

'What are the main problems with an all-male grope?'

Thus begun, the interview ran steadily downhill for several minutes with everyone accidentally falling over *doubles entendres* on the way. However, a discussion of sorts was eventually committed to tape, and it remains a fond memory of our association with one of the outstanding British musicians of our generation.

Another joint venture towards the close of the year was with the Camden Concert Society (once sadly misprinted as the Camden Concrete Society), whose chamber orchestra was conducted by another old friend, John Lubbock. Our concert was at the lovely church of St. John's, Smith Square, London, and the occasion was made especially memorable for us by the evening's guest star, Cleo Laine. The omni-talented Patrick Gowers (who writes scores for feature films, composes guitar concertos for John Williams, invents video games, and has played keyboard for the Swingle Singers) wrote some arrangements for Cleo, ourselves and a jazz trio. Cleo, of course, is not only one of the finest singers (we were going to say 'of her kind' but that is absurd: she is unique) but her musical tastes, like ours, cover a very wide range of forms and styles. We later visited Cleo and John Dankworth at their home in Wavendon, where their All-Music Plan is the inspirational setting for almost every conceivable kind of music-making.

The Smith Square concert was the first of three we gave at important London venues during the winter of 1970-1—something even the most sanguine among us could not have anticipated the year before. The third of these concerts, in March, was at the Wigmore Hall—the only time we have performed there. Between these two was the first of what was to become our annual jamboree at the Queen Elizabeth Hall in January. A day or two before this, aware that we were still innocents in the great big world of entertainment, we asked one of the senior stage staff at the QEH if he had any advice he might care to pass on to us. He thought for a moment, and then said that the one certain way for us to slide inexorably from penury into destitution was to put on a concert at the South Bank on a Tuesday in the middle of winter. Well, what an amazing coincidence, we thought: our show was scheduled for the following Tuesday. Be that as it may, the concert was a complete sell-out, with a wonderfully appreciative audience.

Shortly before the Wigmore Hall concert we had at last completed the recording of the *By Appointment* album at Olympic Studios in Barnes, with Keith Grant as engineer. Keith was not too optimistic about the prospects for the LP, but tried to cheer us up by saying we were the finest group that nobody had ever heard of. However, our wonderful artistry finally overwhelmed all his reservations: 'You may be rotten sight-readers,' he gushed, 'but you've got lousy tone.'

III

The summer and autumn of 1971 was a satisfyingly hectic period for us. We filmed for television a version of Peter Dickinson's *Winter Afternoons*—settings of poems by the American poet Emily Dickinson (no relation) for six voices and virtuoso double-bass, with John Amis and Australian director Bill Fitzwater, at the splendid stately home of Dyrham Park, near Bath. We appeared at the Wavendon, Cambridge, Windsor, Nottingham, Rye, and Dartington festivals; did concerts in Spain and Belgium; auditioned for our first light-entertainment spot on television; and generally put ourselves about.

Our radio work during this time included many more *Invitation to Music* recordings, and several appearances on Eric Robinson's popular show. While in studio for one of these we received a painful but salutary lesson in the technicalities of radio-biz. Eric Robinson was known by reputation but not by face to one of the King's Singers, who shall be nameless (but bears an astonishing resemblance to Nigel). While we were recording with the producer, Barry Knight, the nameless one, not being required for a particular song, went into the production box to listen. While he was there, Eric Robinson entered the box and made various useful

A publicity photograph for our first London concert by the 1970-78 vintage King's Singers.

suggestions to the production team. Now the great advantage of chatting in the box is that nobody on the studio floor can hear you (unless you use the two-way speaker). On the other hand, every word uttered in the studio is clearly audible in the box. So there was a rather sticky moment when our anonymous countertenor rejoined us in the studio and announced: 'There's a fat man with a cigar throwing his weight about in the production box.' Such errors are made only once.

The trip to Spain was a singular experience. It was to take us to Ávila (about 60 miles west of Madrid) on a Saturday evening. We booked seats on a Friday evening flight to Madrid, but the plane was delayed and we landed at about one o'clock in the morning. We had no Spanish money, no hotel reservation in Madrid, and there was no arrangement for us to be met. It looked as though we were going to have to sleep *al fresco*. However, after we had hung about the airport lounge for some time wondering what on earth to do, we began to have the feeling that we were being observed. After a moment, a rather sinister-looking man slid out from behind a pillar, walked quickly over to us, and muttered 'Kingsinger?' in the soft ingratiating manner of one about to offer you dirty postcards. We established our credentials. He glanced to left and right to see if the coast was clear, then drew a bulky envelope out of his coat pocket. It *is* dirty postcards, we thought. But no—it was bundles of pesetas of high denominations, most of them in so advanced a state of disrepair as to give new meaning to the term 'filthy lucre'. Our little group was now joined by three other men who, we feared, were going to mug us but who turned out to be riding shotgun for the cashier. At last, having crossed our palms with (presumably) our concert fees and travelling expenses, the Spaniards vanished into the night.

We dashed off to the nearest hotel and, after 'sleeping fast' (in Pierre Boulez's vivid phrase), we took a train to Ávila—a lovely mediaeval walled city in the mountains of southern Castile. We arrived during the siesta and the entire city seemed to be silently snoring. We found the church where we were booked to perform, and on a notice board outside was a poster announcing our concert—a poster so wrinkled and dusty that it seemed to belong to some event in the distant past. In the evening we changed into our tail suits and walked to the church. The streets still seemed to be lifeless—but to our astonishment, the church was filled to capacity. The audience seemed to have arrived from nowhere and after the concert, which they evidently enjoyed, they melted away.

The whole Spanish episode had a trance-like quality, amusing in recollection, but unsettling at the time. Our Belgian trip soon afterwards was altogether more business-like, and paved the way for many future visits. On this first occasion we appeared at Louvain in a concert promoted by Radio Brabant under the auspices of that arch-anglophile Karel Aerts.

Our audition for television took place at York in November before the veteran producer and talent-spotter, Barney Colehan, who motored over from Leeds. Things had started to go wrong the day before, while we were rehearsing for a concert at Bradford. Al complained of stomach pain, which was quickly diagnosed as appendicitis, and he was carted off to the Royal Infirmary. So we performed as a quintet at Bradford, and had to do the same at the audition. Barney remembers climbing several flights of stairs to an unspeakably dreary cafeteria, sitting down to wait for us, and wondering what in heaven's name had persuaded him to come all that way to listen to five-sixths of an act he had never heard of. However, he was good enough to describe the audition as 'magic', and he signed us up at once to appear on *The Good Old Days*—then already in its nineteenth year on television. This was the only audition the King's Singers ever had: by the time Barney had finished exposing us at the City Varieties, home of *The Good Old Days* in Leeds, we had well and truly attracted the attention of the media. (The fact that we had impressed Barney with only five singers made us wonder if we might not save money and give Al his cards; but then we remembered that his legal training was useful when it came to scrutinizing contracts, so we decided we had better hang on to him.)

'But What Do You Do For A Living?'

During the next few months we were to take some momentous decisions about our careers. Hitherto, in spite of the steady increase in the number of our concerts, radio spots, and other public appearances, the group had taken up only a part of the working life of each of us. However serious our musical offerings might be, our stage manner—the throwaway remarks, the undergraduate humour, our moderately well-groomed (as opposed to calculatedly scruffy) appearance—seemed to our audiences to smack of that uniquely British conception, the 'gifted amateur', rather than of the ambitious professional. We lost count of the number of times that members of audiences came up to us after concerts and, after praising the show, inevitably came round to the question, '...yes, but what do you do for a *living*?'

This could, of course, be taken as a compliment. One of the strengths of the group from the very beginning has been its ability to create an informal, relaxed atmosphere even in programmes of serious and often 'difficult' music. This quality is not, as it were, 'in the script'; it is simply the way we happen to go about presenting a concert. But it certainly derives from our shared conviction that music must engender delight, as pure sound, before it can move one to tears, or laughter, or any other heartfelt response; and such delight often comes more readily to the listener who feels relaxed and at one with the performers.

To get back to our semi-professional status: a decisive step into the future was more or less forced upon us by our friend and ally, David Booth Jones. He sent one of our tapes to an organization called Musicaviva Australia, in Sydney, New South Wales, and it fell on fertile soil. Musicaviva's administrator, the late Regina Ridge, and its president, Kenneth Tribe, wrote offering us a 35-concert tour of Australia and New Zealand in April to June 1972.

This was our biggest break yet, and a wonderful opportunity to lay the ground-work for an international career. But ought we to do it? It would, of necessity, change our lives: if we were going abroad for three months, each of us would have to give up his own job (still the main source of our individual incomes, in spite of the group's success). And when we returned we would have to make ourselves totally available as a group in order to attract sufficient bookings to keep the wolf from the door. It was a crucial decision, but we needed little time to make up our minds.

That being settled, and the Australasian tour accepted, we were faced with another problem. Our existing agent, Christopher Hunt, had done an excellent job for us so far and was a good friend to each of us, but his interests and experience were mainly in the field of classical music. Our repertoire of lighter music had been steadily growing over the past couple of years. And, more to the point, now that we had decided to become full-time professionals we needed to be represented by one of the larger organizations, which would be able to open doors into every branch of musical show business.

It so happened that an ex-choral scholar friend, Patrick Collin, had joined a firm of solicitors, one of the partners in which, George Constantinidi, was also a director of the Noel Gay Organization, the theatrical and light music agents. The firm's founder, Noel Gay (Reginald Armitage), was the composer of such world-wide hits as *The Lambeth Walk, Run, Rabbit, Run*, and *Leaning on a Lamp-post*. He had been succeeded by his son, Richard Armitage (who had himself been a student at King's College), and it was via this rather complex route that we eventually arranged a meeting with him. He seemed to find us tolerably pleasant, and expressed an interest in the possibility of representing us.

That first meeting was at the beginning of January 1972. Later that month we had our annual concert at the Queen Elizabeth Hall. It was a good opportunity for Richard and his staff to decide whether we were a saleable commodity or whether they were in danger of landing themselves with a lead pudding. The programme included our usual mixture of madrigals and songs, but it was greatly strengthened by two specially commissioned works. The first was Richard Rodney Bennett's *The House of Sleepe*, a setting of a passage from Ovid's *Metamorphoses*, which was to become one of the most admired of our more serious pieces. The second work was Carl Davis's *Shakespeare Sequence*, which included settings of a sonnet, a song (*Where the bee sucks*), and an entire scene from *Much Ado About Nothing*, for which Carl enlisted the talents of Ronald Eyre, who had recently produced the play at the Aldwych Theatre. The concert went well—and Richard Armitage agreed to take us on.

Two events occurred before our departure for Australia that encapsulate the mixture of the homely and the glamorous that characterized our career in those days. The first was our concert to 'celebrate' the winding-up of the Airedale Music Society—a sad yet joyous event in the acoustically splendid Victoria Hall at Shipley in Yorkshire. The second was when we worked in his recording studio for the first

A family gathering on the lovely roof-garden of Alastair's flat in Parliament Hill.

time with George Martin, who is best known to the public as the 'fifth' Beatle. He was perhaps one of the few men who could have handled the full spectrum of our repertoire on records. George has this extraordinary recording studio that (for acoustic reasons) is literally suspended from the walls and ceiling of the top floor of a department-store building at Oxford Circus, and resembles the control centre of some vast, futuristic spaceship. We were, alas, to make only three records with him—the *French Collection*, a Christmas album, and a selection of pop standards. His company, AIR, then split from EMI, and we had to decide in favour of our developing relationship with EMI.

And so, even as part-timers, we had come quite a long way already. Ahead of us lay—what? This kind of leap into the unknown may sound fairly romantic. But for us the immediate future was encrusted with the more mundane but pressing problems of mortgages, supporting families or other dependants, and so on. At first, however, these worries were pushed aside by preparations for our tour of the Antipodes—a journey that would absent us from our nearest and dearest for three long months and would involve us in an itinerary and schedules beyond anything we had experienced before. Never mind! In April we set off for Auckland, green as grass but eager to please.

'Six Healthy Englishmen'

I

After a brief stopover at Singapore we landed at Sydney to change planes, and were astonished to see a vast concourse of journalists milling about. Who would have thought that so many photographers and reporters would bother to turn up at six o'clock in the morning just to catch a fleeting glimpse of six young men who, at that time, were quite unknown in Australia? Who indeed? They had come to welcome Mick Jagger, who had travelled in the sharp end of our plane!

We reached Auckland after a total of 36 hours in the air. There seemed to be nobody to meet us until we spotted three gentlemen having a rather unfruitful conversation with six Dutch students. The welcoming committee had spotted these young men together, had jumped to the obvious conclusion – and were beginning to wonder why six Cambridge graduates had such a tenuous command of their mother tongue – when we made our presence known to them. And so we met the first of what was to become a very large number of very good friends in New Zealand. We were taken to our hotel, where we tumbled into bed and slept for 15 hours. Or rather, five of us did: Tony forgot to turn off his television set before collapsing into sleep and was woken, four hours later, by the sound of gunfire. Jet lag clobbered us on our first day, and it took another two days to get our internal clocks fully adjusted.

The New Zealand leg of the tour was sponsored by the Chamber Music Federation. Each town has a music organization affiliated to the federation, and it was members of these local organizations that were our wonderfully hospitable hosts at each point on the tour. Our first concert was at New Plymouth, about 170 miles

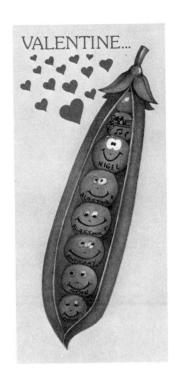

Fan mail at last!

south of Auckland—a short hop by plane—and we were immediately faced with a potentially disastrous crisis: no music stands! This was resolved by one of the committee members, who simply went home and constructed six elegant and practical stands. (A couple of years later the Japanese—who else?— produced stands that are handsome and also light enough for us to pack with our luggage).

Our New Plymouth audience gave us a heart-warming reception and the committee a delightful post-concert party, thereby setting two precedents that were to be observed throughout our tour of this beautiful country. There was, in fact, only one problem of a musical nature that worried us during our first few recitals. The Chamber Music Federation was just that—a body devoted to the promotion and appreciation of classical music; its staples were recitals by pianists, *lieder* singers, string quartets and so on. Small-town audiences at such concerts in New Zealand—as anywhere else in the world—sometimes confuse seriousness and solemnity: they are there to appreciate works of art, but not to be 'entertained', and certainly not to have fun! And so, when we included, at the end of otherwise entirely serious programmes, a few comic songs and sea-shanties, the response was at first equivocal, if not exactly hostile. This phase soon passed. We knew we had turned the corner when a committee member overheard two ladies conferring after one of our lighter sets: 'Do you know,' anxiously whispered one, 'I'm rather afraid I *enjoyed* that!'

From New Plymouth our tour took us to Wanganui, Palmerston North, and big-city Wellington. From Wellington we flew to Timaru, mid-way down the east coast

We spent a whole day walking round Hyde Park with these lovelies, with the intention of advertising Singapore Airlines. Ironically, it remains one of the very few airlines with which we have never flown. It was, however, at Singapore Airport that Brian had the following extraordinary conversation:

Brian: May I speak to Mr Moore (local impresario)?
Answer: I'm afraid he's out. Can you ring in the morning?
Brian: No - we're flying on to Australia. Can I leave a message?
Answer: No, I'm afraid I don't speak English.

of South Island. Our plane on this occasion was a Douglas DC-3—that venerable work-horse one more usually sees in Hollywood films of the mid-1930s. (We did not know then of its legendary reliability, but we deny spreading the rumour that it has to be serviced not by mechanics but by archaeologists.) At all events, the plane's startling antiquity and the fact that we landed in a meadow rather than on tarmac inspired Tony to call across to Simon, 'The big time at last!'—not realizing that Simon was sitting beside the president of Timaru Chamber Music Society. As Al staggered off the plane, bruised but not broken, he was heard to murmur, 'What must a DC-1 have been like?'

Our tour of South Island took in most of the main towns. We especially remember the Englishness of Christchurch and the Scottishness of Dunedin. Our recollections of Nelson that year are now overlain by our experience there on our second tour in 1975, when we were firmly sat upon by Cyclone Alison. From Nelson we crossed Cook Strait again to Wellington, then sang in Hastings, near Hawkes Bay, Rotorua, Hamilton and finally Auckland.

Although this bald statement of our itinerary makes it sound hectic, we managed in fact to spend many hours of relaxation in the company of our various hosts, who went to endless pains to make us feel at home. Typical of such time off was the day Simon spent trawling for trout with new-found friends on Lake Tarawera, near Rotorua. He fished with such success on a supposedly barren stretch of water that it was promptly dubbed 'Carrington's Reach'. (Note by five King's Singers: if you believe fishermen's tales, you'll believe anything.)

Our last week or so in New Zealand was tinged with anxiety. We had commissioned from Malcolm Williamson (now Master of the Queen's Musick) a new work that was to be given its premiere in Sydney. After streams of telegrams had winged their way to and fro across the oceans, the manuscript arrived three days before we left Auckland—and only ten days before our Sydney date. The package seemed rather small, and to our chagrin we discovered that, to save postal charges, Malcolm's publishers had photographically reduced the manuscript to a size in which the notation was unreadable except with a high-powered microscope. So then it had to be enlarged page by page, which cost more precious time.

Our port of entry into Australia was Brisbane, where we spent our first evening with the secretary of the Queensland branch of Musicaviva, Chris Gargett. (Her husband Peter, like most of the King's Singers, loves vintage cars, and it's a moot point whether envy or admiration was uppermost in their minds when he took them down to his garage and unveiled six ancient Rolls-Royces in various stages of restoration.) Brisbane gave the group its first taste of the big international hotel – this was 1972, remember – comfortable, efficient, air-conditioned, and boasting all the approved amenities like vibro-massage parlours and saunas. We have stayed in quite a few by now; they are wonderfully convenient but destitute of atmosphere except for the faint odour of high-denomination travellers' cheques. The Brisbane concert was well received by all, with the exception of a violent tropical storm, which had been refused admission and spent much of the evening trying to blow the building down.

After performing in Canberra, we moved on to the big one—our concert in the Town Hall of Sydney, a vast Victorian pile with an auditorium seating 3,000 people. In order to create an intimate atmosphere, a small stage had been erected half-way along one wall of the auditorium, and the seats grouped around it. So there we were, broadcasting live over the national radio network, and unable to see more than a fraction of the audience in the hall. When Regina Ridge, Musicaviva's administrator, came to see us during the interval, we asked her how she thought the concert was going. She replied that she hadn't heard a note—but hastened to add that she had been outside counting the takings of the programme sellers.

Our apprehensions about the concert were groundless. The audience was enthusiastic, and on the following day Maria Prerauer of the *Sunday Australian* gave

Work at that stage in the development of the Sydney Opera House was so far behind, that guided tours of the building were no longer possible. On the day on which they made an exception for us, presumably because they knew that we would one day sing there, they also made an exception for the family of Nelson Rockefeller, perhaps they thought he would buy it!

us one of the best reviews we've ever had. Characterizing us, a trifle coyly, as 'six healthy Englishmen', she wrote:

> It's a long time since a concert was such fun—and such great art—as the King's Singers' Sydney début...They leap easily from the heavily sacred to the most profanely light...one minute as quirkily and eccentrically English as a furled umbrella in sunshine, the next as swinging as a West End night joint...Effervescent platform personalities...inborn sense of style and professional good taste.

We had four more major concerts ahead of us, at Adelaide, Melbourne, Perth and Darwin, but before then a number of engagements in the smaller towns. This proved to be a delightful interlude in which we made lots of friends and had the chance to see something of rural New South Wales and Victoria. From Sydney we drove over the Blue Mountains to Bathurst and Orange, and then our itinerary took us south and west. Our spare-time activities are now little more than a kaleidoscopic blur: the ancient engine pulling our train to Bendigo bearing a plaque certifying that it had run one million miles—and choosing that day to expire; the lovely Barossa valley, where we undertook research into the vintage; the road-side restaurant in Tasmania featuring a chief's special called 'Vienna Shitzel'; our encounter with a live emu—compared with which Rod Hull's friend is a demure and bashful flower.

In Adelaide, our departure point for the flight to Perth, we looked over the Festival Theatre, which (like the Sydney Opera House) was still being built. The concert hall at Perth was also awaiting completion, and we began to get the feeling that our visit to Australia had been made a few months too soon.

Our last port of call was Darwin, the remote capital of the Northern Territory. The 1600-mile journey was by the milk-run, which touched down at various points *en route*. We took off from Perth at ten o'clock at night and arrived, sleepless, at eight next morning, emerging from the plane into atmospheric conditions of about 500 per cent humidity. At our hotel in Darwin we collapsed in rooms vacated a few minutes previously by the crew of Concorde, then on its less than triumphant sales trip around the world. We slept until the early afternoon.

The concert that evening was unique in our experience. The hall itself did at least have the advantage of being complete. It was made of corrugated iron, which in addition to being painful to the eye has curious acoustic properties. Determined to set an example in this ex-outpost of empire, we turned up looking extremely suave in immaculately pressed tail suits. To complete the sense of incongruity the audience sat in shirt-sleeves, slaked their thirsts with prodigious draughts of Swannies and Fosters, smoked cigarettes, took photographs and dandled babies on their knees. Most of them seemed also to have brought dogs with them; these were tethered in packs outside the hall, and spent much of the evening howling at the moon. It was, in short, a pretty informal occasion, but after they had got over the risible aspects of six men in tail suits, the audience gave us a marvellous time. The whole affair took wings, and for us it was a delightful way to end our first Australian tour. (We returned to Darwin in 1975, only four months after the Christmas Day cyclone had ripped the town apart. The hotel where we had stayed on our first visit was a heap of rubble; all that remained of the concert hall was a slab of concrete; whole areas of the town had been razed. In spite of being offered incentives to move elsewhere, most of the people of Darwin were determined to stay and rebuild the city. Their wonderful spirit was unforgettable.)

Back in 1972, however, Darwin was our departure point for home. According to Tony (who appears to travel with a pedometer strapped to his ankle) the total mileage of our Australasian tour came to 31,000. It had been an exhilarating experience, but we were homesick and longing to get back to Blightly. As we took our seats on the plane, a splendidly plummy Oxford voice invited us to fasten our seat-belts. In our somewhat over-excited state, and after becoming accustomed to the drawl of the Pommy Bashers, it sounded insupportably comic, and we collapsed into hysteria.

The area in which this photo was taken is called, appropriately, King's Park. In the background is the city of Perth, Western Australia.

Home and Abroad

I

Coming home to our wives, families and friends was a joyful experience, but we had little time to relax. We were almost immediately involved in a mini-tour of concerts at Cheltenham, Birmingham, Canterbury, and Nottingham—all in one week and in that order! The rest of 1972 included recording sessions with George Martin, television work, an appearance at the Edinburgh festival, a tour for the Scottish Arts Council and much else.

That 'much else' included a High Court action against a miscreant rabble known as 'Simon Carrington and Others'. What had happened was that, the previous year, we had made our *By Appointment* album for the Chandos Music company, and our contract with them stipulated *inter alia* that we must not record anything for anybody during the first twelve months of the agreement without offering it first to Chandos. In July 1972—three weeks before the end of that first year—we recorded a television commercial for De Kuyper cherry brandy at George Martin's studios. At that time, as we have seen, George had close affiliations with EMI, and it seems likely that Chandos, on getting wind of the fact that we had been working in George's studios, must have concluded that we were making a record for EMI. At all events we had an injunction slapped on us, restraining us from doing any recording for anybody other than Chandos for eighteen days.

It was a fairly harrowing experience at the time, especially for Simon, who had to appear before a judge in Chambers. It all arose from our lack of experience in contracts and from our assumption that everyone was as reasonable and straightforward as ourselves. That this may not always be the case became apparent on another occasion when we did a concert at Cambridge. To our great pleasure we were presented with a cheque on the evening of the concert; to our great displeasure we discovered a few days later that the cheque had been stopped. The negotiations for this concert had been with an organization called RMA. During these negotiations the individual at RMA with whom we had been dealing changed his name to Barrie Hawkins. It was he who signed—and later stopped—the cheque. When we complained, Mr Hawkins said that RMA, not he, owed us the money; later he asserted that RMA owed him money and that he was disinclined to pay us until RMA had settled with him.

Enter Al, solicitor. Since it seemed a straightforward matter of 'suing upon a contract', Al undertook to conduct the case and to appear in person on our behalf. He spent many interesting hours in the law courts in the Strand buried under mountains of legal bumph, with writs and summonses whizzing in all directions overhead. After a great deal of obstruction Al obtained judgment for the full amount against Mr Hawkins.

No doubt these experiences are commonplace among performers in the entertainment field. But they taught all of us to be very wary of putting our signature to documents. Even if you do not fall victim to the trip-wires of legal jargon you are likely to come a purler on the banana skins of the small print. Since Al's triumph he has taken over responsibility for scrutinizing our contracts and other legal papers. He has done us proud—apart from his extraordinary failure to get luncheon vouchers written into our agreements.

Our Edinburgh concert, at the Freemasons' Hall, was memorable in being our first 'live' broadcast from a major festival. It started with a crisis: the concert programmes did not arrive until a couple of minutes before we were due to go on the air. Alastair McIntyre (Al Hume's uncle), who was the senior announcer for the BBC in Scotland, was to introduce the programme. He began reading the notes he had prepared, but then the festival director, Peter Diamand, appeared backstage and insisted that the concert must not begin until every member of the audience had had the chance to buy a programme. 'Backstage' at the Freemasons' Hall consists essentially of a long narrow passage. At one end of it stood Alastair McIntyre, waffling expertly into the microphone while giving us urgent signals to get ready; at the other end stood Peter Diamand forbidding us to begin until the programme money was safely in the coffers. We were stuck in the middle, shaking with fear, and praying that these two super-powers would come to an accommodation. We received the go-ahead a few minutes later, and the concert was warmly received—but we really don't need that kind of excitement to get our adrenalin flowing.

The Scottish Arts Council tour was the first of many for that admirable body, which has done so much to promote up-and-coming artists. Our itinerary included the McRobert Centre at Stirling University where, after the concert, two young Americans asked us why we wore tail suits to perform in. We had not, until then, given the matter much thought: tails were, after all, *de rigueur* for classical

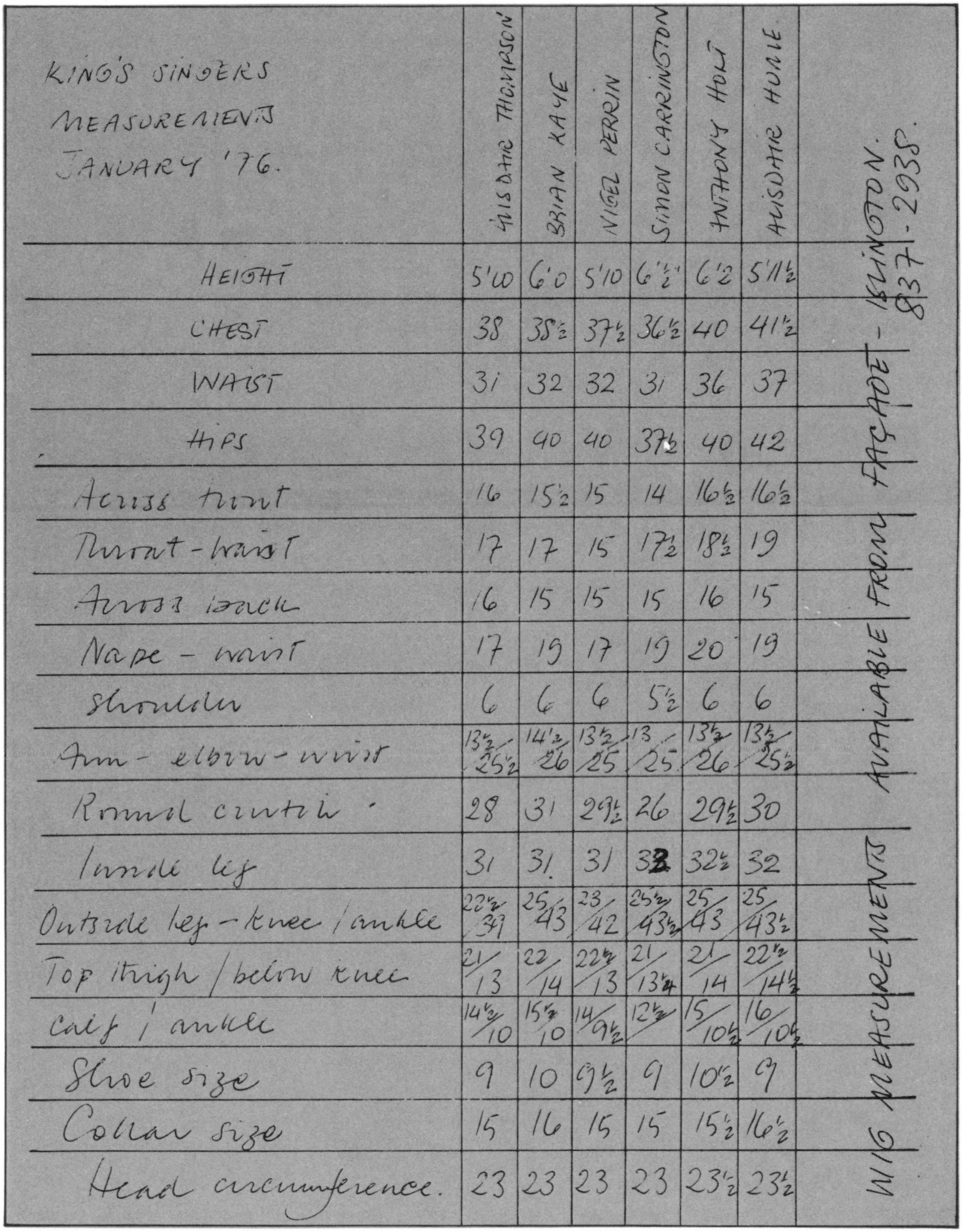

KING'S SINGERS MEASUREMENTS JANUARY '76.

	Alisdair Thompson	Brian Kaye	Nigel Perrin	Simon Carrington	Anthony Holt	Alisdair Hume
Height	5'10	6'0	5'10	6'1½	6'2	5'11½
Chest	38	38½	37½	36½	40	41½
Waist	31	32	32	31	36	37
Hips	39	40	40	37½	40	42
Across front	16	15½	15	14	16½	16½
Throat-waist	17	17	15	17½	18½	19
Across back	16	15	15	15	16	15
Nape-waist	17	19	17	19	20	19
Shoulder	6	6	6	5½	6	6
Arm-elbow-wrist	13½/25½	14½/26	13½/25	13/25	13½/26	13½/25½
Round crutch	28	31	29½	26	29½	30
Inside leg	31	31	31	32	32½	32
Outside leg-knee/ankle	22½/39	25/43	23/42	25½/43½	25/43	25/43½
Top thigh/below knee	21/13	22/14	22½/13	21/13¼	21/14	22½/14½
Calf/ankle	14½/10	15½/10	14/9½	12½/	15/10½	16/10½
Shoe size	9	10	9½	9	10½	9
Collar size	15	16	15	15	15½	16½
Head circumference.	23	23	23	23	23½	23½

WIG MEASUREMENTS AVAILABLE FROM FAÇADE - ISLINGTON. 837-2938.

A measurement chart produced for the Dutch TV film, *We Are Not Amused* – nor are we when we consider how time has changed some of the statistics.

musicians. We asked our visitors what they thought of them. They said they were an 'absolute gas'—an essential element in our comedy routines! Well, of course, we could now either go the whole hog and fit ourselves out with fright wigs and red noses, or we could set about finding suits that were both stylish and sufficiently eclectic to go happily with our increasingly varied repertoire and audiences. After a long search, we eventually found ourselves at the establishment of Mr Arthur Davey, theatrical tailor, of Frith Street, Soho. He quickly sized up our problem, made some sketches of three-piece suits, suggested a good quality blue cloth that would stand up to the kind of hammering we customarily give our clothes, and would hang out quickly after spending hours in a suitcase. We asked him to go ahead, and we wore the suits for the first time at our Queen Elizabeth Hall concert in January 1973. Although we are being paid absolutely nothing for this testimonial, it behoves us to say that Mr Davey's suits were not finally discarded until after our tenth anniversary concert in May 1978.

Early in 1973 we returned, for the last time, to David Booth Jones's Hale Park (David was shortly to move to another lovely house, in the Close at Salisbury). We were there to shoot scenes for Ian Engleman's BBC TV documentary about us, *Six Healthy Englishmen*. We filmed various scenes with our families (giving rise to a short-lived legend that we were six gentlemen of quality who had turned a baronial hall into a plutocratic commune); and we also shot a sequence in which the young composer Paul Patterson took us through rehearsals of his *Time Piece*, a work that had been commissioned for our concert at the Camden Festival in March. The idea of being filmed at rehearsal was a good one, and possibly an eye-opener for our audiences. But it created a problem in that, for several years afterwards, every organization that booked us asked for *Time Piece* to be included in the programme.

During the first three months of 1973, between our many concerts, we recorded a series of promotional jingles for Radio Oxford, then setting up as one of the BBC's new local stations. The jingles were composed by Gordon Langford and recorded by Humphrey Carpenter, an old friend from our student days and now perhaps best known for his biography of J.R.R. Tolkien. In much the same vein we appeared on BBC TV's *Nationwide* to render the newly introduced VAT regulations in the form of an Anglican chant. Many people thought then (and still do) that we were the group that some years previously had had a huge hit with similar treatments of the Highway Code and the weather forecast. Not so: the only begetters of this brilliant idea were the Mastersingers (four masters at Abingdon School), whose chantings were produced by George Martin. They later became good friends of ours and for that reason—and also because we don't like expropriating the good ideas of friend or foe—we were reluctant to commit the idea to tape. In the end, however, we changed our minds; and in 1978, when the BBC changed its radio wavelengths, we chanted the bad news to the nation.

The *Six Healthy Englishmen* programme was first televised on Easter Saturday; it was later to be shown all over the world, and it did a marvellous job in introducing us to an international public. On that Saturday, however, we were *en route* to our second major overseas tour—South Africa. The decision to accept the tour was not

In the middle of a very busy week, we trailed all the way down to the famous ring of ancient stones at Avebury, Wiltshire, to have this photograph taken. It's just as well that we took the trouble as, of course, the exact spot is instantly recognizable.

lightly taken. Many of our friends, who detest the idea of apartheid as much as we do, urged us to decline the invitation. In the normal way, all our decisions are made on a democratic basis by means of a vote. This was one of the very few occasions when we have introduced a veto clause into our rules: it needed just one 'No' vote for us to refuse the tour. We all took time to make up our minds. Simon, for instance, initially opposed the trip, but he eventually changed his mind after reading an article by Lawrence Gander, the exiled former editor of the *Rand Daily Mail*, urging artists to keep open the lines of communication with South Africa. None of us regrets our decision to go, and the success of the tour enabled us to stipulate, for our second visit in 1977, that most of our concerts should be before multiracial audiences (for our third tour, in 1980, all the audiences were to be multiracial). We don't regard this as a particularly wonderful achievement, but it's a small step in the right direction.

In 1973 there was no television in South Africa, so few members of our audiences had ever heard of us, even in the big cities. In the country areas it was uphill all the way until we introduced a more light-hearted element into the programmes. We were able to hear many examples of the haunting music of the Bantu, and the black school choirs put us in mind of the beautiful Maori singing we had listened to in New Zealand.

II

Most of that summer was devoted to festival concerts at Aldeburgh, Edinburgh, King's Lynn, Cambridge, Belfast, Lisbon and Brussels. We also suffered the embarrassment of our first double-booking. It happened during the change-over from our old agents to our new, and we discovered at the last moment that we had contracted to perform at Bryanston School (Dorset) at 8 p.m. and to appear in a cabaret at Goodwood House, near Chichester, at 11 p.m.

We did not want to disappoint either audience; we did not wish to be sued for breach of contract; we needed the money. So we overcame the dilemma with a certain amount of ingenuity. We caught an early train from London to Bryanston, where we had a leisurely rehearsal. At the end of the concert we walked straight off the stage and into two helicopters, which had landed on the cricket field. Lift-off was at 10.05 precisely, and an unexpected bonus was the champagne provided at no extra cost. We flew the sixty-odd miles to Goodwood House in fifty minutes. We landed on the great lawn (the only other people who have been allowed to land there by helicopter are members of the Royal Family – but, after all, we *are* the King's Singers!), walked through open french windows, on to the stage, and did a cabaret act.

Well, we earned our double fees that night. On the other hand, helicopters are more expensive than buses (or at least they were in those days). The pleasure of the Goodwood show was greatly enhanced for us by the presence in the audience of Barbara Kelly, who had planned the evening's entertainment. We were to spend some delightful hours with Barbara and Bernard Braden. These two Canadian expatriates know more about the top close-harmony groups than most, and they offered us a lot of good advice about musical material and how to use it, for which we have remained extremely grateful. Bernie always visualised us playing the lounges at Las Vegas with great success, but we have not yet had the opportunity to prove him wrong!

Our dramatic arrival at Goodwood House.

In November and December we made our first tour of the United States. Shortly before our departure we appeared for the first (but by no means the last) time on BBC TV's *Pebble Mill at One*. Also on the programme was the man who appears to have discovered the secret of eternal youth—none other than the Sultan of Snip, Vidal Sassoon. When we told him we were just off to North America he insisted that we drop in for the full treatment at one of his recently opened salons, in New York, San Francisco or Toronto. When we eventually turned up in San Francisco—one of the most beautiful cities in the New World—our American agent Mariedi Anders was anxious to take us sightseeing on our only free morning.

'Where would you like to go first?' she asked.

'Take us,' we commanded, 'to Vidal Sassoon's.'

Thinking that jet-lag had curdled our faculties, Mariedi humoured us and took us to the salon. Well, none of us had experienced anything quite like this before. But that night we walked out onto the stage looking, as Brian remarked, absolutely heavenly (his actual words were, 'like nothing on earth'!)

Our tour took in Halifax (Nova Scotia), Cambridge (Mass.), where we sang at Harvard University, Toronto, then down to Nashville (Tenn.), Springfield (Miss.), Ames (Iowa), Washington (D.C.), where we sang at the Library of Congress, San Francisco, Waco (Texas), Oshkosh (Wis.), Gainsville (Fla), Quebec and Montreal. If you look at a map and follow this itinerary from place to place, you will say that it's insane—and you will be right. But that's how the bookings worked out, and we greenhorns had to follow them.

Our American experience has been fascinating and frustrating. The United States is, of course, the biggest musical market-place in the world, and we have attracted some really marvellous reviews in most of the great newspapers over there. On the other hand, we have yet to beg or browbeat our way onto any of the significant television shows, which is essential if we are to make a real breakthrough. To date we have made six tours, each one better than the last, but none quite as epoch-making as we might have hoped.

Among incidental pleasures of our first tour was a visit to the Grand Ole Opry in Nashville, where we heard Roy Acuff, Tex Ritter, Tammy Wynette, and the last-ever performance by the legendary Stringbean. (On his return home that night Stringbean and his wife were murdered, apparently for the vast quantities of cash they had lying about the house, Stringbean never having bothered much with banks.)

The year closed for us with our first visit to Belfast for a concert in St. Anne's Cathedral. Perhaps because, in those days, so many overseas artists were declining to perform in Northern Ireland, the cathedral was jam-packed and the audience gave us one of the warmest and friendliest receptions we have ever had. A highlight of the

Even if the name *is* incorrectly spelt, the thought is there! This was an improvement on the normal signs which hang outside such establishments, where we have read such gems as 'Your host with the most from toast to roast' and 'If you want to improve the world, start with yourself'! We also saw one once, which boasted, 'We're the number one.' Unfortunately for them, they had missed out the apostrophe!

visit was the post-concert party at the Deanery (now a regular feature of our Belfast trips). Guests at the party are expected to sing or entertain in one way or another, and most people present seem to have an out-of-the-ordinary talent. We King's Singers have an inflexible rule against doing stand-up numbers on informal occasions of this kind; but the rule is enthusiastically flouted at the Deanery party. The climax of the entertainment that year was a most beautiful version of *The Keys of Heaven* by the Archdeacon, Graham Craig, and his wife Bertha. They could obviously have made a successful career as professional singers had not Graham had a vocational commitment to the Church—not to mention a reckless passion for cricket.

The year 1973 saw the release of *Out of the Blue*, the most successful record album of our first decade. By our tenth anniversary in 1978 we had made 20 LPs; all of them sold well, and *Lollipops* and the *Madrigal Collection* have been exceptionally successful. But *Out of the Blue* went like a winner from the start and has continued in the same vein. We have often been asked why this should be and the general feeling is that it embodies most successfully exactly what we are and what we do on the stage or television.

Nana and After

I

So we moved into the second half of our first decade—not with a bang but a misprint. Our first concert in 1974 was in the now vanished Priory Theatre at Whitley Bay in Northumberland, which was presided over by Hubert Dunkerly, an octogenarian ex-Carl Rosa baritone. The concert was greatly to the liking of the audience, who no doubt were as surprised as we were to read in the *Shields Weekly News* that they had been listening to 'six young women with remarkable voices ranging from deep bass to high countertenor'. No one was more delighted by this gaffe than Ron Goodwin, who (you may recall) had composed *What Kind of Things Do the King's Singers Sing*? He worked the following couplet into a revised version:

> He thought we were ladies, it gave us a fright;
> He must meet his lady friends very late at night!

The following month we made our second tour for the Scottish Arts Council. Evidently word had got about concerning the success of our first. At all events, at Dumfries 600 people crammed into the hall—on Burns' Night! The following morning a local paper praised our facility in almost any foreign language, and damned our impudence in coming to Scotland and mispronouncing the words of *Auld Lang Syne*. The following day we sang at the Ayr Music Society and when they heard that we had sung to 600 in Dumfries, they rapidly tried to turn their 400-seater into something rather more impressive! In the middle of a set of church motets a jumbo jet took off from Prestwick Airport nearby (Brian later called it an 'Ayr-plane'—but he'd had a busy day). We had already announced the Latin title of the next motet, and we had to wait for about half a minute until the roar had died away before giving the English translation: 'Men of Galilee, why stand ye staring up to heaven?'

The pace of our professional life was increasing all the time. We had reached that stage in our career when we seemed to be spending as much time on promotion—personal appearances, preparing publicity material and so on—as on making music. If approached in the right spirit, this kind of thing can be fun; it is, in any case, a necessary part of making one's way in show-business. And there's the rub: ever since our first Australasian tour we had been undergoing a gradual metamorphosis from 'classical musicians' into 'entertainers' (or 'mere entertainers' as one critic called us). This transformation was less welcome to some of us than to the others. It was implicit in our increasing range of venues and audiences and in the broadening of our repertoire; it was visible in the ways we presented our material—our stage act, if you like—which we were beginning to tailor according to our audiences and programmes. Over and above all this was the simple fact that we were busier than we had ever been before. On a fairly typical day in February, for instance, we spent a hectic morning being photographed in attractive or off-beat settings in and around London; in the afternoon we were in EMI's Studio 1 recording an album of madrigals; and in the evening we moved over to Studio 3 to record a series of vocal effects for an album by the singer/songwriter Colin Blunstone.

On another occasion we had a date in Belgium followed a day or two later by a visit to Cardiff for a show on Welsh television. The Welsh producer wanted to include material on our methods of preparing for a concert, but on the day when he wanted to film us rehearsing we were booked aboard the ferry to Ostend. So it happened that a Welsh camera crew shot scenes of the King's Singers 'rehearsing' in the grounds of Dover Castle in the pouring rain and then boarding the ferry. We never discovered if, or how, this material was stitched into the television show. The implication that the King's Singers invariably rehearsed in the rain, and that they assumed the normal way to get from London to Wales was by taking ship from Dover, may well have nourished our reputation for eccentricity.

II

The year included visits to Holland, our second tour of America, several appearances on Scottish television shows, and recording TV commercials. We also had the excitement of a sell-out Hallé Prom at the Free Trade Hall in Manchester. But our outstanding experience of 1974 was our appearance as guests on all six programmes of *The Nana Mouskouri Show* for BBC TV. Steve Race's *Invitation to Music* had brought us to the attention of a large radio audience; Nana's show introduced us to a truly international television audience. Even today, interviewers all over the world still refer to it.

Each programme was recorded on a Monday at the Shepherd's Bush Theatre in London. We wondered at the time if we had been chosen because we were the only singing group that happened to have six consecutive Mondays free. In fact, of course, our stint on each show involved much more than the Monday. Each Thursday the show's producer, Yvonne Littlewood, the musical director, Peter Knight, Nana, her Athenians group and ourselves would meet to decide on our particular contributions to next week's show. The choice for our solo spot was no problem, as by now we had a large and varied repertoire. The difficulty arose in choosing the one or two songs we would sing with Nana and her guests—as often as not in Greek! Peter Knight would then spend the rest of the day (and much of the night) doing arrangements of the songs, and we would meet the following day to sing them through.

We invariably had concerts on the Saturday and Sunday, often in distant parts of the country, but we would reassemble at Shepherd's Bush on the Monday and record the entire programme by heart (it was before an invited audience). This

Getting our own back on Nana Mouskouri, with James Galway helping us to teach her *Phil the Fluters Ball*!

presented a considerable challenge to us. As choral scholars and classical musicians we were accomplished sight-readers, and there had rarely been any need for us to learn anything by heart—and never at the speed required for this show. It is a fairly general rule among musicians that one is either a good sight-reader *or* a good learner-by-heart — one is rarely both. It was tough at the time, but that brief but intense course of learning at speed was to prove an enormous benefit to us, and we have retained the ability ever since. (Incidentally, having courageously attempted to sing in Greek on this series, we took hideous revenge on Nana when she invited us to appear on her 1976 shows. On one of these we shared the guest spot with James Galway, and to maintain the Irish flavour we forced Nana to learn Gordon Langford's unspeakably complex arrangement of *Phil the Fluter's Ball*, which is tricky enough to sing in its unvarnished version. To our chagrin, Nana sailed through it effortlessly.)

Our happy affair with Nana in 1974 did not end with the delightful dinner she gave us and (so far as we could tell) the entire television staff engaged on the shows. Some weeks later we met in a recording studio to complete an album of songs that included many of the arrangements that Peter Knight had done for us. (Peter, like other top-notch arrangers, works the sort of hours that would send most people to an early grave. One night we were at a dinner given by Moira Anderson at her home in Glasgow after we had appeared on her television show. Peter, who was the show's musical director, was there and as usual was the life and soul of the party—until half-way through the dessert course. At that point he simply keeled forward, laid his head on the edge of the table, and was fast asleep in five seconds flat. Moira, who was familiar with Peter's work-rate, didn't bat an eyelid.)

In the UK the effect of our appearance on Nana's shows was immediately apparent. In the twelve months from September we performed no less than 200 concerts—a wildly extravagant programme and one that today we could not hope to emulate. By the end of that twelvemonth period the King's Singers had quite definitely arrived as far as British audiences were concerned. We were not only playing to full houses in larger theatres than ever before; it was evident that we were attracting a new kind of audience. Thousands of people coming to our concerts for the first time were expecting to hear the same kind of light-hearted music as we had performed on Nana's shows. It would have been pointless to have stuck to predominantly classical programmes, waiting until the last set of songs in a two-hour concert before providing the kind of entertainment that most members of the audiences had come to hear.

It must not be thought that we allowed ourselves passively to 'go where the money is' or that we diluted the quality of our concert programmes. Trained as we were in 'serious music' idioms, we had begun our career, and achieved our first critical successes, with programmes of essentially classical music. But even in those early days, as we have seen, we had sought to show our audiences that classical music need not be taken too solemnly and had included sets of 'jollies'—some glees or close-harmony standards. Each of us, of course, has his own musical preferences; but our collective test of a song's quality—classical, pop, whatever—has always been whether or not it is good of its kind and whether or not we enjoy singing it. If it fails on either count, it doesn't get into the repertoire.

The development of our concert programmes in the 1974-5 period represents a change of emphasis rather than submission to the demands of showbiz. Our concerts during that time certainly included an increasing proportion of the more popular items; but on many occasions they also included pieces of quite 'difficult' contemporary music that most newer members of our audiences might normally have taken pains to avoid. The interesting thing is that, more often than not, these latter works were received just as enthusiastically as the popular numbers.

III

Our second American tour, in the autumn, began in the east, taking in Halifax, Sackville (New Brunswick), Dartmouth College in Hanover (New Hampshire), Schenectady (N.Y.), Yale University in New Haven (Conn.), and Hunter College (N.Y.). As can be seen, we were concentrating on college audiences, which seemed to be the sector of the American market that we should try to consolidate first. Unfortunately we were not, on this occasion, on the exciting student-promoted circuit: our bookings were made through the official bodies at each university. We got an early inkling of the no-expense-spared quality of life at North American universities at Sackville, where the stage equipment had to be seen to be believed. When we suggested that the stage was somewhat vast for the six of us, someone at a console pressed a few buttons and the walls and ceiling crept in upon us until we had an area of optimum size.

After each concert we would have a friendly get-together with the students and faculty members. The only thing that marred these receptions was the habit, so deeply engrained it might be an article of the American Constitution, of confining the refreshments to Hawaiian punch and cookies. On such occasions we are always panting for a pint, preferably best English bitter. It must be admitted, however, that the average American beer would have served our needs scarcely better than the punch. Americans are invariably shocked at the English love of 'warm' beer. The typical Milwaukee brew is served at temperatures measurable only on the Kelvin scale; swallowing it is a purely tactile sensation—which is just as well because, compared with 'real ale', it is destitute of flavour. (Let it not be thought that we would have liked to tour America in an alcoholic daze. Although advertisement hoardings were constantly beseeching us to 'Drink Canada Dry', we decided that this was a job for the natives.)

Another aspect of travelling in America was our difficulty in getting used to the central heating in hotels: let it be placed on record that at Hanover Tony discovered that the furniture in his room was actually hot to the touch. Remember, we are six healthy Englishmen. In winter we expect to wake in the morning to icicles in the wash-basin and rime on the coverlets. Actually, there was more to it than this. The combination of central heating and air-conditioning tends to play hell with our vocal chords. In Poughkeepsie (N.Y.) it was enough to give Simon a throat catarrh. He went to see an ear, nose, and throat specialist, who lived in a vast mansion set in several acres of rolling parkland. Pushing the doorbell with one hand and fingering his wallet with the other, Simon wondered what on earth he had let himself in for. The doctor was full of understanding, but very brisk: in one apparently seamless movement he peered down Simon's throat, wrote out a prescription, and presented a bill for $200, payable in cash.

One of the most enjoyable moments of this tour was our meeting in Schenectady with the president of the Society for the Preservation and Encouragement of Barbershop Quartet Singing in America—that passionately dedicated community of lawyers, bankers, insurance executives, doctors (and even, no doubt, a barber or two) who devote their spare time to acquiring expertise in this exciting form of amateur music-making. We also encountered what SPEBQSIA members call a 'tag' man—an expert coach who teaches three other singers the parts of a tag (musical phrase), which the quartet then rattle off with a unique blend of precision and gusto. After one of our concerts this tag man taught three of us the parts of a rather complicated phrase, and there was a rather embarrassing moment when we got our bits right and he fluffed his!

We also had the pleasure, after our concert at Yale, of being invited by the director, Fenno Heath. to spend the rest of the evening at the Glee Club Room—the nerve centre of male-voice singing groups the world over. We were entertained with great generosity, and the Whiffenpoofs (notwithstanding most of them were about to sit exams) gave us some unforgettable music. Later we sang to them, standing beneath the portrait of Marshall Bartholomew.

The Hunter College concert was our New York City début. It was one of a prestigious classical series that are broadcast live on Sunday afternoons; not exactly Carnegie Hall, but a good platform for us. We were greatly heartened to see Cleo Laine sitting in the stalls (she was drawing wildly enthusiastic audiences at the St.Regis hotel). Apart from her, the audience seemed to consist largely of rather ancient ladies, most of them in the cheaper seats towards the back of the hall. After our first song there were cries of 'Louder!' from several of these ladies, while a considerable number of their more daring sisters stood up and shuffled towards the various unoccupied seats nearer the front. Heaven knows what this mixture of bellows, pounding feet, and squeaking seats must have sounded like to the radio listeners.

The second stage of the tour consisted of another visit to Waco (Texas) followed by concerts mainly in the West Coast states. Our itinerary again resembled the meanderings of an alcoholic earwig across a map of America. In spite of our exhaustion, however, we felt we were beginning to take the temperature of this great country and even to make something of a name for ourselves—until we got to Los Angeles. As soon as our plane landed we phoned the lady who was promoting our concert there. The conversation went something like this:

'Well hi there! Welcome to L.A.!'

'Thanks very much!'

'Now tell me, have you brought your own instruments?'

'Actually, we don't use any instruments.'

'Is that so? And will you be using our piano?'

'We don't use a piano either. It's just us and our voices.'

'Why, isn't that *sweet*!'

'We hope so.'

'Well have a nice day.'

When we met her later we asked about the series of concerts of which ours formed a part. She was curiously vague about it, but it finally became plain that the concerts were attracting negligible audiences—so negligible, in fact, that she had decided to miss our performance and go to a Gilbert and Sullivan show instead. We wondered for a moment whether she had fallen under the spell of some new cult specializing in alienation therapy. No such luck! But the day was saved for us by the presence of Neville Marriner (then conductor of the Los Angeles Chamber Orchestra). After the concert Neville invited us back to his amazing house, which is famed both for its staggering array of electronic devices and for the fact that Harpo Marx once performed there.

Consolidation

We now pass fairly rapidly through 1975. It was, in fact, a very good year for us: the mixture much as before, only more of it. Music festivals were proliferating all over the country, and we performed at no less than seventeen of them (at King's Lynn we had the pleasure of singing to, and meeting, the Queen Mother, for what was to be the first of several occasions, culminating in the Royal Variety Performance). In April and May we made a second tour of Australia and New Zealand, and in the autumn we had another three weeks' hard labour in the United States. This included our third visit to Waco, Texas, in honour of which the Mayor named 17 November 'King's Singers Day' in Waco, and presented us with a certificate proclaiming the event. We made three more albums and appeared frequently on radio and television.

Musically the most interesting and rewarding feature of the year for us was our involvement with the Nash Ensemble, which included many musicians who had been contemporaries of ours at Cambridge. The connection centred mainly on concert performances and a recording of a new work, *Requiem for Father Malachy*, which John Tavener had written for our combined forces.

The saddest and most moving occasion for us in 1975 was the memorial service for Michael Flanders, at which we sang Donald Swann's beautiful setting of *Bilbo's Farewell* and part of Michael's and Jo Horovitz's *Captain Noah and His Floating Zoo*.

CITY OF WACO, TEXAS

Office of the Mayor

Proclamation

I, __L. Ted Getterman, Jr.__, by virtue of the authority vested in me as Mayor of the City of Waco, Texas, do hereby *Proclaim*

__Monday, November 17, 1975__

as

__"KING'S SINGERS DAY"__

in the City of Waco, and urge each and every citizen of our City to __extend a warm welcome to the King's Singers__ as they again thrill Waco audiences with their musical excellence and warm British wit.

In testimony whereof, witness my hand and the Seal of the City of Waco this the __17th__ day of __November__, A. D., __1975__.

_____
Mayor, City of Waco, Texas

Attest:

_____
City Secretary

'We (and Audiences Everywhere) Are Not Amused'

An entry in Brian's diary for 1 January 1976: 'The plan this year is to spend less time away from home.' This was certainly a heartfelt wish, especially of Brian, Nigel, Tony, and Simon: they all had young families who were growing up, for good or ill, seeing their fathers too seldom. Moreover, as a group we were confident enough in the demand for our services to have become a little blasé, and even to complain of overwork. Our problem was that feeling common to any established performer who has worked hard and has successfully launched a career and is beginning to wonder whether the future, however profitable, is going to present exciting new challenges or will simply follow a familiar groove.

Two weeks later, Brian wrote this entry: 'It looks as if we are going to be busy after all.' This turned out to be the understatement of the year—January and February were among the most hectic months of our career, and they involved some radically new departures to keep us on our toes.

The first of these novelties was working with Greg Lake (of Emerson, Lake and Palmer). Greg had got to know our music well towards the end of 1975 through his musical director, Godfrey Salmon, a friend of ours from Cambridge days. Each member of ELP was recording tracks on his own (their plan was for each to contribute one solo side to a double album and to combine forces on their fourth side) and Greg used us as a special effect in his song *Closer to Believing*. He also required us to stand in front of the microphone for what seemed like several hours singing the word 'humbug' over and over again. This was in fact the only word in a song of the same name (if the lyric writer was on piece rates he had a lousy deal—unless he got royalties for repeats). Greg then had the extraordinary notion that we should accompany ELP on their forthcoming world tour. Six soberly dressed Englishmen singing madrigals amid fireworks and psychedelic lighting at Madison Square Garden might have been fun—or hell. It never happened because we were, in any case, committed elsewhere. But we enjoyed our brief association with Greg, during which he arranged and recorded our single of the Lennon/McCartney *Strawberry Fields* and opened our eyes to new concepts in the production and performance of pop standards.

Perhaps the Queen of the Netherlands (then Crown Princess Beatrix) and Prince Claus had never met a countertenor before!

We next embarked on a series of visits to Holland. Our first engagement was a charity concert at a private house in Blaricum, near Amsterdam, before a select gathering including Princess Beatrix, as she then was, and her husband Prince Claus. We rehearsed there in the afternoon, then went for dinner to a favourite restaurant nearby, having ascertained exactly when our act was to begin. We had a delightful, leisurely meal and strolled back to our dressing rooms. We had timed our return to coincide with the last few minutes of the performance of Marco Bakker, the only other artist on the bill. In fact, there was a deadly hush in the house, interrupted only by those rather special coughs and rustling noises that betoken an audience that is waiting for something to happen and is not keen on waiting much longer, if it's all the same to you. Evidently there had been a last-minute change of plan, the royal couple had a subsequent engagement, so the concert had started early—but what on earth had happened to the English gentlemen? We flung on our performing gear, took a deep breath, and dashed on stage.

Our next two engagements in Holland were to be on Wilhelm Duys' television chat show and to film our version of David Bowie's *Life on Mars* for the Dutch equivalent of *Top of the Pops*. Then came our most ambitious excursion yet into television: we were invited to make a film that was to be the Dutch entry for the 1976 *Prix d'Italia*, the major European television award.

The film was called *We Are Not Amused* and was in six episodes, in each of which one of us played the part of a monarch who is the victim of assassination. The fact that the monarchs in question were Frederick the Great, Queen Victoria, William the Silent, Louis XIV, Ivan the Terrible and Queen Elizabeth I indicates the serious nature of the project, not to mention its dogged adhesion to historical fact.

As things turned out we had two of the busiest and most hilarious weeks of our lives. We rose at six in the morning and had to spend about two hours in the make-up room. (Let's face it, apart from the noble brow, Brian's resemblance to Good Queen Bess is not obvious at first blush; and while Al is virtually Queen Victoria's double, he took ages to get her mittens on.) We would film all day until about six in the evening, have dinner, and then stay up until midnight tossing around ideas for the next day's shooting. An eighteen-hour day every day for a fortnight is fairly shattering, but the work was fun.

A few titbits:

The Ivan the Terrible episode was a send up of that marvellous, dark, death-bed scene in Eisenstein's film. Simon, as the expiring tyrant, had to loll about on his magnificent bed (upholstered orange-boxes – no expense spared), while the rest of us, got up in the habits of Orthodox priests, mimed to a disgraceful pre-recorded spoof of the Russian *Kontakion*. At the moment before death, when an opened Bible was about to be placed over his face, Simon had to lift himself on one elbow and mutter 'We are not amused' in Russian. The remark, it goes without saying, had to be accompanied by vigorous rolling of the eyeballs. It so happened that Simon was a recent convert to contact lenses and was still trying to get the hang of them, so that the eye-rolling resulted in the lenses either popping out or trying to force a passage into the roof of his skull.

Al as Queen Victoria, Tony as John Brown with four would-be assassins. Nigel (far left) as a foam-soaked Frederick the Great.

Clockwise from top left: Alastair as William of Orange; Brian as Death in the Louis XIV sketch; Nigel as a flute-playing Frederick and Alastair (with double-bass) as J.S. Bach.

Clockwise from top left:
the haunting of Louis;
Simon as Ivan the
Terrible; the grand finale;
and Al, Alastair and Brian
as three poisoned priests
in the Ivan sketch.

The part of the assassin, Balthasar Gerards, was played by Nigel (type-casting, do we hear?). Gerards was in fact the killer of William the Silent; in the film he had to kill all the other monarchs as well—the producers arguing cogently that he might well have murdered them too if he had had the chance. Nigel's principal task was to appear at the climax of each episode on a sinister black stallion. Now, Nigel excels in many things; for instance, he outstrips almost everyone in sheer incompetence aboard a horse. An entire morning passed while Nigel attempted to coax his steed through the gates of the Prinsenhof in Delft, where William the Silent (A. Thompson) and the Burgomeister (A.Hume)—heedless of their peril—were playing skittles with oranges on the top of an enormously long table. No sooner would the horse pass through the gates than it would be confronted by the fearful vision of Tony (a palace guard) clad from head to toe in armour. As Tony clanked forward to take the reins, the horse would forget its lines and make for open country.

Tony, indeed, had rather poor luck with horses all round. As Louis XIV he had to ride a horse across the studio, up a ramp, and on to a mock-up of the Sun King's throne. The horse, upon realising the hazardous nature of its role, demanded danger money and, when this was refused, made a token demonstration in the middle of the studio floor. A problem now arose as to who was to clear the mess away. A score or more studio technicians insisted that they were eager to volunteer, but felt bound to point out that by doing so they might violate demarcation agreements.

The final episode took place on the beach at Bergen-an-Zee, near Alkmaar. All six monarchs appeared together each carrying his or her national flag, and they were immersed in a mountain of aircraft foam. Although the scene no doubt caused the stoniest-hearted viewer to dash away a tear, at the time we were more concerned with the fate of the microphone man. He had to lie on the sand just out of shot and reach out with his mike so as to record everything we were singing. As the foam rose, he gradually disappeared until, by the end of the take, only the tip of his mike was visible, like a U-boat periscope. The Russian judge was so overcome that he had to leave as his national flag was covered in foam by six irreverant Englishmen.

The finished film was, in the eyes of most critics, a right royal turkey. It was certainly amusing neither to ourselves nor, so far as we can discover, to anyone else. The fun was in the making of it. It was certainly a refreshing experience for us as it involved not only singing but acting and dancing too. We regard ourselves as pretty passable hams, and as for dancing. well, casting all modesty aside, we make the Incredible Hulk look pretty flat-footed.

Germany; Poland; Australia

I

We had a short rest after we returned from Holland, and then we embarked on something new: a self-promoted tour of England. Hitherto, as we had begun to establish a reputation, we had rarely declined invitations to perform, first on the music-club circuits or later on the broader-based commercial promotions. As our diary of engagements became ever more crammed, we discovered to our astonishment that promoters weren't in business to present only King's Singers concerts. The result was that, in order to fulfil contracts and keep busy, we found ourselves having to dash all over the country, logging up hundreds of miles between engagements. On one occasion, for instance, we had concerts on consecutive days at Huddersfield (Yorks), Holyhead (North Wales), and Sherborne (Dorset). If we'd had an executive jet at our disposal it would have been no problem; as it was, such journeys were exhausting and would ultimately have affected the quality of our performances.

So we decided to plan our own tour, promoting concerts at venues that, as far as possible, made geographical sense. The tour included concerts at a number of big halls whose managers had expressed an interest in us and the whole enterprise was co-ordinated by our agents, the Noel Gay Organization. The northern part of the tour took in Bradford, Preston, and Liverpool (a sell-out concert in the Philharmonic Hall on our first appearance in the city). The southern part, preceded by a useful promotional spot on London's Capital Radio, began at Fairfield Hall, Croydon. Until then we had shunned this hall in view of its size and on the assumption that, if we had any fans in the area, they would come to see us in London. We were quite wrong: the hall was full, with a lively and appreciative audience; and it's been the same at all our subsequent concerts there.

Our audiences had been smaller than we had hoped at Bradford and Preston, and we had anything but full houses at Brighton (the Dome), Portsmouth (Guildhall), Bristol (Colston Hall), and Cardiff (New Theatre). We were learning the lesson that self-promotion is a risky undertaking unless you have a man on the spot in each town who is adept at the kind of publicity that will attract local audiences. There followed the midlands part of the tour, with somewhat better houses, followed by Manchester, Glasgow and Perth.

Our appearance in Manchester furnished another example of the perils of self-promotion. We had contracted (or so we thought) merely for an afternoon's recording session of brief inserts that would later be fed into various programmes on Radio Piccadilly. We had taken a morning train to Manchester and arrived in time for a quick bite of lunch at the studios. While waiting to use the telephone, we overheard a lady asking at the reception desk for a ticket for the King's Singers concert. Somewhat alarmed, we asked the lady to which concert she was referring, and it turned out that our studio session was, in fact, to be a full-scale in-studio show performed before an audience. We had about thirty minutes in which to devise a programme. Shrugging off the crisis with enviable composure, which we cleverly disguised as blind panic, we plundered some titbits from our forthcoming Glasgow and Perth concerts, and went on the air.

II

In mid-summer of 1976 we made our first visit to West Germany. The country has a unique musical heritage: almost every town has a concert hall offering hospitality to excellent local or national music groups before large and enthusiastic audiences. We had fancied our chances there, especially with the classical end of our repertoire, ever since our earliest days – but until now the doors had seemed closed to us.

Our German record company had arranged an appearance on a television show to be filmed in Hamburg. It was not an auspicious occasion. Our spot consisted of three sixteenth-century German *lieder.* That was fine—except that we were followed immediately by another, rather different group—the electrifying Surprise Sisters rocking away in their skin-tight gold hot-pants. Our dismay at this curious piece of programme planning was tempered only by our relief at having sung before rather than after the ladies. Later in the year we returned to appear on the popular *Lieder-zirkus* television programme, sharing the bill with the rapidly ascending French rock singer Julien Clerc, Ralph (*Streets-of-London*) McTell, and Gisela May, the fabled interpreter of the Brecht-Weill canon. Our songs were more suited to the occasion this time, and included Daryl Runswick's mind-blowing arrangement of *Obladi Oblada*(even today this version, when announced on one of our shows, produces a *frisson* of anticipation among several of our regular followers, who are convinced that sooner or later it's going to pitch us toes over tonsils). Our initial assault on Germany lit no bonfires; but it was a start, and more—a very great deal more—was to follow.

Soon after our return to England we did three concerts in the West Country, in the course of which we were paid one of the most glowing tributes in our experience. During the interval of our show at the University of Exeter we were besieged by six students—all of whom, by a curious coincidence, asked us to include in our last set of songs Richard Rodney Bennett's arrangement of Randy Newman's *Dayton, Ohio*. Luckily, we had planned to sing it anyway (it was a favourite with our audiences at the time)—but it was nice to be asked. The next day we had lunch with our good friends on the staff at Dartington Hall. As we were relaxing over coffee, in walked the six students from the previous evening. Amid an expectant hush, they proceeded to give a carbon copy of our version of *Dayton, Ohio*. They had taken the trouble to write down the notes of the six parts from our recording, and at the concert they had made a careful study of our stage performance, down to the smallest gesture. We were dumbfounded, thrilled, and flattered: it was like seeing ourselves perform for the first time.

Later that summer we recorded a King's Singers' *The World of Music* show for BBC TV with producer Yvonne Littlewood. It was a magical experience to be hosts

Opera scena with Dudley Moore.

of our very own show—so magical, in fact, that we did not quite believe it until we were shown to Dressing Rooms 1 and 2 at the Shepherd's Bush Theatre instead of being stuck away somewhere on the third floor. Our guests, certainly, were of star quality: Marisa Robles, the harpist; Michela Kirkaldie, the Australian ballerina (then having a tremendous success in *The Merry Widow*); and Dudley Moore who, a day or so before the show was due to be filmed, dashed off a tragic *opera scena* for ourselves as orchestra and himself as an authentically lunatic prima donna.

III

After a short break we ventured forth on our first visit to Poland, to appear at the International Festival of Contemporary Music in Warsaw. We had been invited through the good offices of the Polish composer Krzysztof Penderecki, who was on the festival committee and had already written music for us. We were to make up the second half of a concert, at which we were preceded by a string quartet that nudged and picked its way through a couple of pieces so *avant-garde* they were beyond the horizon.

We sang four works. Richard Rodney Bennett's *The House of Sleepe* was a good starter: a serious and beautiful work, it was politely received. Penderecki's *Ecloga VIII* (settings of Virgil) followed, and was greeted with the sort of restrained frenzy suitable to a festival of this kind. Our third piece, Luciano Berio's *Cries of London*, was pretty light-hearted by comparison; but Berio is a very hot number on the international circuit so this piece, too, got a good hand.

Now came the crunch. Our last work was Paul Patterson's *Time Piece*. It was only after we had tasted the flavour of the festival at the beginning of the concert that we realised we had boobed. *Time Piece* is, in our view, music of a high order; but it is blatantly entertaining and, worse still, is in parts hilariously funny. It was too late to swop it for something heavier, so we crossed our fingers, burned our boats, took a deep breath, and socked it to them. For a few moments the members of the audience sat frozen in silence, wondering whether to believe the evidence of their ears. Then a few of them began to look cautiously at their neighbours, and one by one facial expressions that had been rehearsing displeasure began to melt into smiles. Gradually, the whole audience seemed to relax, to sink back into their seats, and to abandon themselves to enjoyment. At the end there was tumult—we thought they would never stop clapping and shouting. They demanded an encore. Perhaps a madrigal or so? Not a bit of it. The festival director himself demanded a lollipop, so we went back and sang *I Only Have Eyes for You*. The response was rapturous. And that is how the International Festival of Contemporary Music stumbled into Tin Pan Alley.

After the concert Penderecki took us to a large hotel for dinner. Now, on such occasions dinner cannot be allowed to proceed without almost continuous bending of the elbow in toasts to—well, everything from peaceful co-existence to the neatly turned ankle of the waitress. On this occasion the choice of weapon was schnapps (vodka being employed merely to quench our thirsts). People may tell you that schnapps is a near cousin to gin; that may be so, but it seemed that night to be closer kin to nitro-glycerine. The toast was given, the schnapps was downed in one gulp, and the top of one's head flew off. This went on for several hours; or, rather, we expect it went on for several hours—our recollections are hazy.

IV

October 1976 was a fiendishly busy month for us. It included a two-week consolidation tour of Australia, where we sang in all the main centres, sandwiched between brief television stints in Holland and West Germany.

The Dutch prelude was a trip to Amsterdam to film two songs for the Martine Bijl programme. Then we boarded our jumbo at Schiphol airport and flew on to Australia. We gave concerts in the largest halls in Perth, Hobart (Tasmania), Adelaide, Melbourne, Sydney, Canberra, and Brisbane. These major shows were interspersed with others at some of the smaller towns where we had enjoyed especially good receptions on our previous tours in 1972 and 1975. The tour, although fairly brief, was exceptionally exhausting. Apart from the concerts, much of our time was taken up with the business of supportive publicity in the way of press conferences and interviews on radio and television as well as those curious occasions known as 'personal appearances'. (What, by the way, is a non-personal appearance – going around with a sack over one's head and signing autograph books with an 'X'?)

The effort we put into all these side-shows must have been worthwhile, however. All our concerts were filled to capacity with people who remembered or had heard good things about our previous tours. The audiences were wonderfully enthusiastic and in general we felt that our connections in Australia had done us proud.

A remarkable example of audience participation occurred at our concert for the Blue Mountains Concert Society at Springwood (New South Wales). On the day before the concert Les Hodge and Tricia Byrne, two of our friends at EMI Australia, had taken us to dine at the Fisherman's Lodge, an excellent seafood restaurant on the waterfront at Sydney. A few hours before the Springwood show Tony began to realise that last night's oysters were fighting back. Like the good trooper he is, Tony manfully kept going through our first two sets of songs, but then he keeled over on our dressing-room table and in a strangled voice declared he was unable to move.

We could, of course, have lashed him to the table and held it upright on the stage, but kindlier counsels prevailed and we decided to ask if there was a doctor in the house. The response was electrifying. Springwood appears to be eastern Australia's breeding-ground for physicians; better still, all of them seem to like our music. Before we had time to say, 'Tell us where it hurts,' the dressing-room was overflowing with them, all looking slightly sheepish without their white coats and little black bags. By some miracle they managed to get Tony well enough to rejoin the concert. How they did it became a matter of fevered speculation on all sides. Some claimed the trick had been done by dangling a photostat of a Sydney surgeon's fees before

Tony's eyes; others believed he had received intravenous doses of Lamingtons, a celebrated local confection reputed to cure everything from athlete's foot to xenophobia. At all events, Tony eventually hobbled back on stage, where he was greeted with the cry, 'The King is dead: long live the King!'

In spite of our hectic itinerary we made a point of looking up as many as possible of the delightful friends we had made on previous tours. Typical of these was the Ingham family, who raise sheep on a vast spread near Orange (New South Wales). The Inghams' son Richard customarily travels to outlying areas of the spread on a powerful Kawasaki Trail bike, and Simon delightedly accepted Richard's invitation to accompany him on a jaunt across the bush on a similar machine. Dark deeds were afoot. Richard set off at breakneck speed, with Simon (no slouch on a motorbike) about twenty yards behind him. They came to a slight mound. Richard disappeared over the other side. Simon followed, and immediately found himself waist-deep in a waterfilled gully. (Richard, having cleverly avoided the trap, was by now disappearing over the horizon, howling with laughter.) Richard's mother, Annie, is a painter (and cattle-breeder, organist, raconteur, printer, *restaurateur*, breeder of beautiful daughters, etc.) and, as such, extremely successful and sought after. On the first visit to the farm, most of us came away with canvases—a recurring habit, as can be seen by scanning the walls of every King's Singer's home!

We six Kings – a glorious moment in the middle of a dance routine – one of the many that have done so much to convince people that we should stick to singing.

The Halifax hangover song, in which we faced the difficult task of imagining that we had drunk too much.

V

We broke our homeward journey for the brief interlude in West Germany, where we appeared on a television show featuring the popular Swedish singer Lil Lindfors. A few days later we found ourselves at Bramham Park, a magnificent stately home between Leeds and York. Here we filmed a Christmas special for Yorkshire Television called *We Six Kings*. Dressed in a variety of lavish costumes we played the parts of King John, Edward VII, Richard III, Henry V, Charles I, and Henry VIII, and sang a programme of Christmas songs. Unlike the ill-fated *We Are Not Amused* it turned out to be one of the most convincing and rewarding things we have done on television. Our one complaint was that, after a fortnight in the heat of an Australian spring, we were now plunged into the chill of a colder-than-usual North Country October, and many of the scenes were being shot out of doors. For collectors of the grotesque we could have recommended the sight of six English monarchs in full regalia clustered in the early morning mist around the film unit's catering van and stuffing themselves with bacon-and-egg butties.

Film and television companies are notorious for the lengths to which they will go to achieve trivially authentic settings, especially in period pieces. One of the songs we sang in this film was *Quem Pastores Laudavere*, a simple sixteenth-century German carol. We filmed it in the lovely Mirror Room at Bramham Park and, although we sang it without any accompaniment, it was thought that if we were gathered around a harpsichord the scene would gain a touch of something-or-other. Whereupon Alexander Skeaping, a famous supplier of these instruments, was asked to furnish us with one of his most expensive and attractive examples. He transported it all the way from London to Yorkshire—and then spent an entire morning tuning it. We did a three or four minute take, leaning elegantly against the priceless instrument, which was then carted all the way back to London again. (Next time we are going to insist on Karajan and the Berlin Philharmonic.)

Our three delightful days ended with the shooting of the closing sequence of the film, in which we rode away down the baronial drive in, or perched on, a magnificent coach-and-four, singing *Deck the Hall with Boughs of Holly*. For one reason and another, including bad light, the scene took hours to set up. Eventually everything was ready, the cameras started to roll and the coach set off down the drive. We had scarcely covered fifty yards when the director Vernon Lawrence, was seen to be leaping in the air, waving his arms, and bellowing, 'CUT!' We were wondering what on earth had happened when, from behind the coach, a lightly steaming muck-spreader hove into view, apparently making a desperate bid for stardom. It was decided that the machine did little for the Dickensian ambience of the scene, and it was certainly not the flavour of the month, so we had to go back and shoot the sequence all over again.

Fiasco Italian-Style

I

There was to be an uncommonly large number of rather special moments—delightful as well as disastrous—before this eventful year closed. One of the most pleasurable occasions was the concert at the Queen Elizabeth Hall to celebrate the fiftieth birthday of our old friend Joseph Horovitz. Our contribution was to sing *Captain Noah and His Floating Zoo* with Jo at the piano, three of the close-harmony arrangements he had done for us over the years and a share of the 'all-star' surprise tribute at the end. We also dashed over to Stockholm for a very encouraging début concert in Sweden; appeared on Tom O'Connor's television show, where we were presented with a silver disc to commemorate the success of our *Out of the Blue* album; revisited Northern Ireland; appeared in concerts at the Royal Festival Hall; and made a short tour of Italy.

The Northern Ireland tour lasted a week. Our first concert was at Londonderry. Each of us travelled independently from London, and we very nearly had to perform as a quintet. Let's be perfectly clear about this: Tony is the very soul of punctuality; it's just that he has a habit of arriving late—especially at airports. On this occasion he forgot to allow for the rigorous and time-consuming security checks on travellers flying to Northern Ireland. He missed his plane at Heathrow and finally arrived at Belfast late in the afternoon. As he looked anxiously around, hoping that someone had been detailed to take him to Londonderry, he was spotted by an alert taxi-driver, who insisted that he was just the man for the job. They drove off at

Rehearsing for Joseph Horovitz's fiftieth birthday concert in the Queen Elizabeth Hall, London, with Geoffrey Simon and the now sadly defunct Australian sinfonia.

considerable speed and Tony—already on edge owing to the missed flight and the general situation in Ulster—began to harbour suspicions as to the authenticity of the driver. His imagination took wings when, in the middle of nowhere, the driver ignored a signpost pointing to Londonderry and shot down a dark country road. 'Don't you worry yer head, sorr,' he explained, 'it's a quicker way.' By now Tony had convinced himself that he would be found, days later, in a disused quarry, and he was squaring his shoulders and preparing to sell his life dearly (in other words, for cash), when the taxi hurtled into Londonderry and deposited him outside the hall a few minutes before the concert was due to start.

At Belfast the cathedral mounted a sort of mini-festival built around our concerts on the first two nights. On the third day we sang at a special lunch at the City Hall hosted by the Lord Mayor, Sir Myles Humphreys (inspiration of the 'Smiles for Myles' campaign); and that evening we sang at a special festival service in the cathedral. By the end of our Ulster week both Nigel and Tony had lost their voices completely. This was something of a disaster because we were due to appear the following night at a charity concert in the Royal Festival Hall organized by the Stars Organization for Spastics. We eventually decided that four King's Singers were better than none and appeared as a quartet.

Bad throats are, of course, the curse of the singer. As will have been apparent, we have been pretty lucky in this respect over the years. The problem is not necessarily due to too much singing. In 1979, for instance, we flew over to Germany for a week of concerts after we had just enjoyed an extended summer holiday. During the second concert Tony's voice began to sound rough, and by the end of the evening there was nothing left at all. He was rushed to a clinic for treatment and by the next day he was able to make a few tolerably musical sounds (Brian: 'Back to normal'). We decided that Tony should appear in the second half of our show that evening, and that we would do the first half as a quintet. At the beginning of the concert the promoter came on stage looking very solemn and wringing his hands. He explained to the audience that Herr Holt had been taken *ernstlich krank* (seriously ill) during the previous evening but that, thanks to the tireless efforts of an entire army of specialists, he might be able to rise from his sick-bed to appear later. Tony duly appeared for the second half, looking atrociously fit and deeply tanned from his recent holiday in the south of France.

II

Our week's tour of Italy was brimful of conflicting emotions and bizarre happenings. We landed at Pisa in the morning and drove about 180 miles to the Umbrian capital of Perugia for our first concert, which was held in one of the city's beautiful art galleries. Other engagements followed in Milan, Trento and Belluno in the north before we came to Rome for the final concert. This turned out to be one of the most gruelling experiences of our career. Our record company in Italy had decided to promote a show at which, they told us, we would appear with one other artist. We enquired as to whom this other artist might be, but the record company became a trifle coy, saying merely that it would be a singer of Neapolitan songs. This sounded all right to us: after all, even the great Gigli had not spurned such material; and in any case, we reasoned, the concert was bound to be a respectable affair because it was being held at the Vatican's Sistine Theatre.

We spent most of the morning in Vatican City recording an interview interspersed with songs from our albums and plugging our concert over Radio Vatican. The concert was due to begin at 9 p.m.; we were making up the second half of the bill and were due on stage at about 10. We spent the afternoon wandering around Rome, ate a leisurely dinner, and arrived at the theatre soon after the concert had begun.

Now, to be candid, none of us can claim to be an authority on the Neapolitan genre, but most of us are acquainted with it from ancient recordings. The sound coming off the stage suggested to us that it had developed somewhat since the old days. We had not realised, for instance, that the singers are nowadays accompanied by electric guitars, or that they serenade their signorinas with strobe lights. One or two of us even ventured to suggest that this sounded surprisingly like rock music—Neapolitan rock music, of course. And although the musicians were far from home, they were certainly making enough noise to have been heard in Naples.

The audience greeted the singers before, during, and after each song with screams of approbation. They seemed reluctant to let them go at the end of the performance but, when the curtain finally stayed down, they repaired *en masse* to the bars.

So then it was our turn. The lights went down, the King's Singers were announced, and on we came in our smart suits, frilly shirts, and bow ties. Our first number was thoroughly in keeping with the spirit of the evening: a merry madrigal—with a fa la la and a hey nonny no! The audience was transfixed: eyes goggled, and several hundred litres of chianti froze in mid-swallow. But this lasted only for a moment. As one man, they conceived it their duty to howl us down and, credit where it is due, they bent unstintingly to their task. We couldn't understand everything they said—they were also stamping their feet and hitting the furniture—but it seemed likely that if we sang *Arrivederci, Roma* and suited action to the word, they would not stand in our way. For our part, we had contracted to sing for forty-five minutes; we decided to do just that, and the hell with it. We were crucified in the madrigals, concussed in *Time Piece*, but fought a lion-hearted rearguard action of pop songs. Our only consolation was that, embarrassing as the experience had been for us, it must have been much worse for the members of our record company sponsors sitting in the stalls!

We were to return to Rome in much happier circumstances in February 1978: a concert in a classical music series before a smaller audience that included many expatriate Britons. But even then the city had something up her sleeve, and the concert was prefaced by an authentic excursion into the theatre of the absurd. When we were announced, we entered through a door set in the middle of the back of the stage. Or, to be strictly accurate, we didn't. The door would not open. We had a whispered conference. 'Try pushing,' someone suggested. We tried pushing: no good. 'Can you see anything through the keyhole?' enquired another. Yes, we *could* see something through the keyhole: the key, which had been inserted from the other side of the door. Well, of course, there was only one thing to be done. We knocked. Eventually a brave member of the audience leapt on stage and, although almost prostrate with hilarity, unlocked the door and bade us enter.

That February the managing director of EMI Italy and his wife took us to lunch at Alfredo's, whose establishment is famed for its sensational *fettucini*. We were attended to by the maestro himself, and he served the managing director's wife with *fettucini* on a silver platter. Then, as if by magic, he produced a golden spoon and fork from a back pocket and told the lady she was to have the signal privilege of using the cutlery presented to him personally, many years before, by no less than Mary Pickford and Douglas Fairbanks. *Mirabile dictu!* So we fell to with a will, feeling very grand and exclusive. A couple of minutes later a party of rich-looking tourists were shown to a nearby table. The lady in the party received her *fettucini* on a silver platter and, as if by magic, Alfredo produced a golden spoon and fork from a back pocket and told her she was to have the signal privilege, etc. Mr & Mrs Fairbanks must have adored *fettucini*!

The year (1976, that is) ended with a concert accepted at very short notice at La Maison du Radio in Paris. The circumstances were curious, to say the least. It seems that the France Musique radio station had found itself with an excess of funds that, somehow or other, had to be spent before the end of the year. So it decided, more or less on the spur of the moment, to hold *une semaine anglaise*, and we were among several British artists invited to take part. What we had not realised was that France Musique had not only to commit itself to this expenditure but had actually to get rid of the money before New Year's Day. At all events, our extremely handsome fees were delivered, in cash, during the interval at our concert. The lady who brought it warned us not to leave it in the dressing rooms, so we tottered on stage for the second half of the concert with our slim-fitting performing suits almost bursting at the seams: Six Wealthy Englishmen.

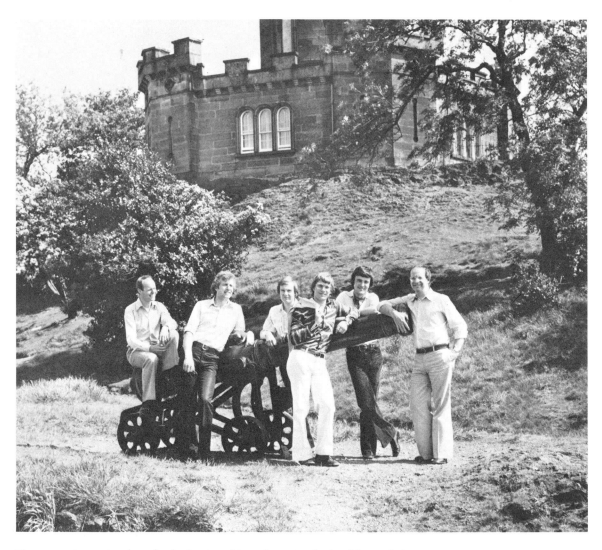

Our experience in church choirs taught us how to deal with can(n)ons.

Points of Departure

I

There were two main strands of thought in our collective mind as we moved into 1977. The first was prompted by that concert on French radio. We had accepted the invitation not only on account of the size of the fee (which was, admittedly, mouth-watering) but also because it gave us our first real chance to win a sizeable French audience. Hitherto, however, we had regarded the week between Christmas Day and the end of the year as professionally 'out of bounds': it was one of the few periods of the year we had invariably set aside for spending with our families.

The French date turned our thoughts towards the whole question of how to sustain a very busy professional career involving much travel while attempting to pursue a civilised form of existence. In our earliest days, of course, we had been delighted to accept every suitable engagement that was offered to us; more recently, we had been able to be more selective in the kinds of engagements we under-took—but the sheer number of bookings seemed steadily to increase. By the end of 1976 we had reached the point where our way of life had, as it were, become self-ratifying: the greater our success, the greater seemed to be the pressure on us to become more successful. The pressure was due not so much to our collective ambition as to a seemingly immutable law of show business. Success, we all felt, was delightful—but when would we have time to enjoy it?

The second strand of thought followed from the first. We began to wonder if we were not becoming a little mechanical in our approach to life and to our work. The group's success was by now far beyond anything we could have anticipated. But everything seemed to be running too smoothly: bookings flowed in, our engagements diary was full to bursting, and we seemed to take even the most ambitious concerts, the most elaborate tours, a bit too effortlessly in our stride.

We needed something to make us sit up and think. It came with a vengeance on 21 January, when Alastair Thompson announced that he wanted to leave the group. It's fair to say that over the years each of us, at one time or another, had harboured thoughts of giving up. But Alastair was the first to make the break, and the shock was very great. It had been tacitly assumed that, if anyone elected to leave, the group would be disbanded: we had been convinced that it would be almost impossible to find, let alone to absorb, a new member once the 1969 line-up had settled down. Now, however, we had come such a long way (we had lasted longer than the Beatles!), and our contractual commitments stretched so far into the future, that it would have been almost impossible to give up even if we had wanted to.

Alastair's generosity eased our problem. He promised to delay his departure until we had had a good chance to find a successor, and someone suggested as a possible

We have appeared on the BBC TV programme *The Good Old Days* many times—this shot was taken in the City Varieties Theatre in Leeds, where the programme is filmed.

time the date of our tenth anniversary concert, which was already being planned for 1 May 1978—about sixteen months hence. This took the immediate pressure off, but we were all immensely saddened at the prospect of losing Alastair. (The sadness was felt just as acutely by our families: soon after the news was announced at Simon's home, his then six-year-old daughter Rebecca—an especially ardent fan of Alastair's—was found weeping quietly over a cup of tea.)

Fortunately, perhaps, our immediate commitments allowed us little time to brood. We started work on completing the album of contemporary pop material of which Greg Lake's arrangement of *Strawberry Fields* had become the guide track. We appeared on three television shows—*Pebble Mill at One*, *The Good Old Days*, and *The Ronnie Corbett Show*. On this last, Ronnie appeared in King's Singers garb and performed magnificently as a countertenor; that is, his tenor effectively countered the efforts of the rest of us. We also made another tour of Scotland. Our friends were enormously impressed when we told them we had performed at Carnegie Hall. We omitted to add that this one was in Dunfermline (we've also made similar mileage from the Albert Hall, Nottingham).

In February we reorganised our system of internal management. In the absence of a group manager, each of us has taken responsibility for one or more aspects of the group's affairs. Nigel, for instance, had started out as 'records and photos', co-ordinating with EMI and organising the sale of records at concerts; when Alastair left, Nigel took over the financial department. Al was known as the chairman: he had been responsible for raising funds for such things as specially commissioned music; he now took over from Brian as business manager, which involved such things as liaising with the Noel Gay Organization to ensure that what appeared in our engagements diary coincided with bookings they had made for us. Alastair was now, and until he left, our librarian—an extremely difficult job that required him to make sure that the various items of our repertoire of a thousand or so pieces turned up in the right place at the right time. After Alastair left we managed to lumber Tony with this; until then he had been treasurer, dealing with things such as the intricacies of expenses and VAT (Tony: 'I cheated—my father is an accountant!'). Simon was the musical link man, explaining our requirements to composers and arrangers, co-ordinating programme details, and researching possible additions to the repertoire. Brian took over Nigel's responsibility for records, photos, and publicity. Major and minor decisions on these and any other aspect of the group's affairs were taken, as always, as the result of a vote by each of us; in case of a tie, we tossed a coin.

II

During the spring we made our second tour of South Africa, where we were pleased to confirm that most of our concerts were attended by multiracial audiences. In box-office terms the tour was an enormous success. Soon after landing at Johannesburg we went to the television studios to record a twenty-five minute show. Television had started in South Africa only two years before; there was still only one channel, but by now most white families had a set. Our show was transmitted at peak viewing time on the Saturday night after we arrived. It served as powerful publicity for the tour, and on the following Monday all of the theatres on our itinerary, including the 2,000-seat City Hall in Durban, were sold out.

By then, however, we had plunged into a crisis. Before filming the show we had a very pleasant lunch in the executive canteen at the television studios. Our hosts warned us that a 'flu bug was going the rounds and asked us if we were troubled by that sort of thing. We assured them that our strict regime of jogging, cold baths, and clean thoughts more or less guaranteed our immunity but that, if the worst came to the worst, we all caught the infection together, lowered our voices by half an octave, and carried on as if nothing had happened. About half an hour after lunch we were lining up the first scene of our show when Tony (good grief, not *again?*) complained of feeling faint, and within a short time it was confirmed that he had caught the bug. During the next couple of days he sat in a crumpled heap in a corner of the studio; whenever the cameras were to roll he joined us to mime his lyrics or to compose his features into a sincere (that is, rictus-like) smile. He staunchly made an appearance at our first three concerts while running a high temperature.

We were booked for two concerts in Johannesburg, but the demand for tickets was so insistent that we had to give up one of our free days to fit in a third. All three, in Jo'burg's vast city hall, were packed to the gunwales. After the second, on a Sunday afternoon, some friends invited us to dine at their farmstead in the evening.

A party at the Ambassador's residence in Cape Town, where Brian played the piano for Anne Zeigler and Webster Booth.

A South African publicity photograph taken outside the new opera house in Pretoria.

They also invited eight members of the Black Orpheus Choir who had been at the concert. After dinner it was their turn to make music. They began, a little tentatively, with their own arrangement of an English folk song. Then they launched into Zulu music. They made a marvellous sound, the haunting tunes and complex rhythms affected not a whit by the singers' prodigious intake of cane spirit as the evening wore on. As we were about to take our leave, the choir and the house and farm workers gathered on the porch and sang us farewell, many with tears streaming down their faces. It was a moment we shall remember forever, but it soon passed. We immediately experienced the embodiment of the fears of our critics at home as we departed in limousines to our hotel while the choir, if they were lucky, caught the last bus back to the cardboard slums of Soweto.

The evening at the farm intensified our already considerable interest in African music. This was to culminate in the commissioning of a work from Lewis Nkosi, the Zulu writer, and Stanley Glasser, a white South African who was Head of Music at Goldsmith's College, London. This work was *Lalela Zulu*, a cycle of six songs. It was first performed in the summer Hallé Proms—the body who had commissioned it—and it quickly became a regular item in our concerts in England and abroad. Meanwhile, we spent a fascinating afternoon with Andrew Tracey (whose show *Wait a Minim* enjoyed such a huge success in the West End and on Broadway). His father spent years travelling in the bush recording the songs of many different tribal groups, and his tapes represent the most important treasury of African music in existence.

As we had done on our first tour, we managed to spend two days and a night in the Kruger National Park, the vast game reserve near Transvaal's frontier with Mozambique. Human visitors to this marvellous wildlife sanctuary sleep in little round, thatched huts within enclosures. As the best time to see the animals is between dawn and breakfast, we went to bed at eight o'clock. The night was full of sounds: the occasional howls of wild dogs, the delicate trampling noise of a herd of elephants on a nocturnal route march through the bush; and unidentifiable rustling, scratching, and creaking noises that interrupted the eerie silence. The next morning's drive was very special. To see every kind of God's creatures roaming free makes one impatient of zoos not to speak of all the restrictions man imposes on his fellows.

Seven o'clock on a chilly evening in early April in failing light is hardly the best time to join the statuary decorating the centre of King's College fountain for a photograph, but it was a unique opportunity for Sir David Willcocks to gather his former flock for a replay of a similar picture years before (see p 14). The occasion was the 1979 annual conference of the Incorporated Society of Musicians of which he was president. The odd men out are Philip Ledger (centre) and Ian Wallace (top right), the incoming president – during whose hazardous crawl back along the ladder bridging the large stone basin of deepish cold water his glasses (not in a case) flipped out of his inside jacket pocket and disappeared beneath the wavelets – his after dinner speech nearly followed them! Hearing his cry of anguish, Brian bravely removed his dinner jacket, stripped his arm to the shoulder and restored the unexpectedly washed bi-focals to their grateful owner. He was thus able to see the imperfections of his speech with unexpected clarity!

THE KING'S SINGERS

Photographed at Kings' College, Cambridge, with the President of the Incorporated Society of Musicians (Sir David Willcocks), the President-Elect (Ian Wallace) and Philip Ledger, organist and director of music at King's.

III

Back in London we completed an album of songs by Flanders and Swann and Noël Coward, and then dashed over to West Germany to make a couple of television recordings in West Berlin and Cologne. The latter was for a popular show called *Plattenküchen*, which was devoted to the idea of putting makers of hit records in bizarre situations. On this occasion the show was built around a running gag involving a large black dog. We had recently released in Germany a single of *Don't Get Around Much Anymore*, in which Brian sang the lead. In the middle of filming it for *Plattenküchen*, the dog trotted over to Brian and cocked its leg against his trousers. This led to a fairly interesting discussion as to whether the dog's action implied praise or censure.

Our next big date was a 'live' appearance on Val Doonican's television show. Live TV is invigorating, especially if something goes wrong; the iron rule, on such occasions, is to continue as if nothing has happened. We joined Val to sing the love Irish folk song *She Moves Through the Fair* and we had just finished the line

'She came softly to me, her feet made no din'

when there was a tremendous bang somewhere behind us in the studio. In perfect unison we rose perhaps six inches into the air, descended, and carried on with exemplary *sangfroid*. We learned later that a floodlight had crashed to the floor behind a backcloth. The light was extremely hot and constituted a fire risk, so one of the technicians had to crawl behind the drapes and drag it out of harm's way. In spite of having badly blistered hands, he was full of enthusiasm for the excitement of live shows.

INTER-OFFICE MEMORANDUM

COMPANY:
TO: **ALASTAIR HUME.**

DATE: **27th July, 1979**
FROM: **RICHARD ARMITAGE**

A really superb bunch of flowers - unhappily not in a satisfactory water situation - arrived here on Wednesday from Mrs. V. Goodbaum - card attached.

Confronted by a choice between removing fifteen percent of them and posting the remainder in 6 different directions or enjoying them myself I selected the latter course and thought of the six of you. I need hardly urge that a note of thanks is sent.

R.A.

A thought from our agent.

94

It was about this time that various people who had our best professional interests at heart began to get a little fidgety about our image. They warned us that we were constantly in the public eye and begged us at all costs to eschew deed or word that—in a phrase that instantly passed into KS folklore—was 'not consistent with star status'. We were not quite sure how people with star status ought to behave (perhaps they jump the queue at Fortnum's tea counter); but we took these strictures to heart. And so it came about that, when we had to give a concert at Southport, we decided to travel in style: Al hired a Rolls-Royce Silver Shadow, and we glided up to Lancashire to the strains of *The Magic Flute* on eight-track stereo. The 'new' us didn't last long, alas. Simon was perhaps the most disgraceful back-slider, arriving for our appearance in the Royal Variety Performance at the London Palladium on a moped.

IV

Our most important engagement of 1977, and one of the most significant milestones in our career to date, was our concert début in West Germany in the summer. We were invited to take part in the music festival held at the stupendous Schloss Ludwigsburg, near Stuttgart. This was an enormously encouraging breakthrough since the festival attracted many of the most influential German music critics; moreover, our concert was to be broadcast several times throughout West Germany over the following months. While we were at the festival we were presented with two *Schallplattenpreis* awards, which are made annually by the German record industry; one was for 'the best classical record of the year' (our *Madrigal Collection*), the other for 'the best international artist in any category' in recognition of our various other albums released in West Germany. These honours and our concert proved to be a wonderful launching pad in what was to develop into one of the most important markets for us outside the UK.

After short tours in Norway, Holland and Belgium we took a break. At the beginning of January we had promised ourselves more time with our families and so, after years of almost uninterrupted work, we awarded ourselves a two-month sabbatical. It was a delightful interlude—a complete rest from singing, from rushing around the world, and indeed from each other. For some of us it was the first time we had spent a really extended period with our children. (It must be admitted that Simon, for whom two months without music-making would be purgatory, dusted down his double-bass and played in concerts with no less than three orchestras; but he, too, had a family holiday in the West Country).

We were by no means 'invisible' during this period, having previously made a stockpile of radio and television material that was heard and shown in our absence. The radio programmes were in the form of a mini-series that was broadcast on Sunday evenings (with repeats on Fridays). It covered a wide range of musical tastes and styles, and we introduced the programme ourselves. It provoked a considerable, and very interesting, response from listeners. Most of our regular followers wrote to say that it was the best use we had ever made of the medium, which was very gratifying

The King's Singers,
c/o B.B.C.
Broadcasting House,
London W1A1AA

Oh dear, King's Singers,

                    I have just written to
cancel our booking for your concert at Rawlins
School in Leicester on January 23rd. 1978, one
of the Leicester Subscription Concerts sponsored
by the Education Department of the County.
      Your early records gave us great delight
and we were delighted to see that you were coming
to Leicestershire, but then........ we heard your
Sunday lunchtime performances!! Why this barber's
shop image? Many of the songs are not suitable
for your voices. My husband, a sculptor, frequently
speaks of 'truth to materials' - I feel that you
have neglected this and feel that anything can be
adapted to your style but it cannot and indeed,
should not! Flanders and Swann were so right for
The Honeysuckle and the Bindweed - your voices
were not.
      It must, of course, be tempting to widen
one's appeal to a larger audience, but it is
braver and more honest to maintain integrity.
I hope that you will listen again to the recordings
of the Sunday concerts and decide that you do not
like the resulting mish-mash (I can think of no
other description).
      Let me know if you decide to change. I
might even renew our application for the
January concert.

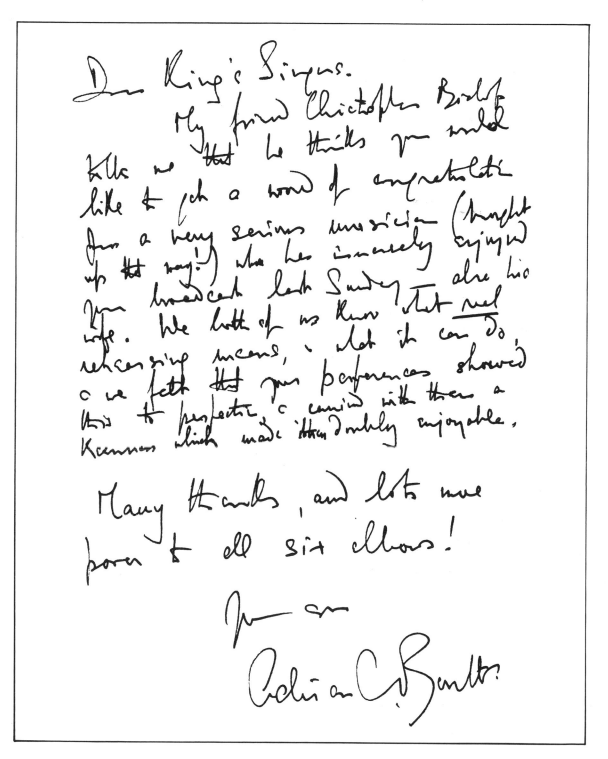

Conflicting opinions on a radio series from a serious music lover and Sir Adrian Boult!

because we thought the same. We were particularly struck by two letters that arrived by the same post. One was from a lady who enjoyed the classical end of our repertoire but who thought we were debauching our talent by pandering to the market for 'cheap' music. The second letter was from Sir Adrian Boult, who wrote to say that the series had brought him nothing but pleasure (which could, however, have been as nothing to the pleasure his letter brought us). In replying to these correspondents, we quoted each one's letter to the other.

Our hibernation ended with an hour-long concert, the opening event of the Three Choirs Festival, which was held that year in Gloucester. The concert was in the cathedral, and we followed it almost immediately with thirty minutes of close-harmony singing before a wine-drinking and extremely enthusiastic crowd packed tight in the cloisters. It was a pretty strenuous way of getting ourselves back into the old routine, but we enjoyed it.

Having spent many years driving to isolated concerts in a motley collection of cars, when we co-ordinated our four week, twenty concert tour of the UK in 1980 – we used a campaign coach. It eased the burden even if we did occasionally suffer from coach lag.

Winding Up the Decade

I

With autumn upon us we had to think seriously about finding a replacement for Alastair. It was obviously going to be difficult. Indeed, we were not at all sure of how to begin the search. For some groups, it might have been possible to advertise ('Tenor wanted: fine voice and clean socks essential', etc.) and to hold formal auditions. For us it was out of the question: we were obviously looking for a fine voice (and, indeed, clean socks if possible); but it was also vital that we should know the person well, that he and we liked each other, that his voice blended with our sound, and that he had the resourcefulness to endure the often exhilarating but invariably exhausting professional life we lead.

After a great deal of thought, and armed with a few strong recommendations from friends whose judgement we trust, we sang with six prospective candidates during the next four months until Christmas. In the end, we were all agreed that there was only one who matched our 'specification' exactly—and that, of course, was Bill Ives.

However, we are leaping ahead of events. In the autumn we recorded our second King's Singers' *World of Music* show, produced by Yvonne Littlewood for BBC TV. Our guests were Chris Harris, with whom we had first worked on one of the German *Liederzircus* shows and who had just had an enormous success in the one-man show *Kemp's Jig* at the National Theatre; and the Romanian pan-pipes virtuoso Gheorghe Zamfir. For us the high spot of the show was our version of the Flanders and Swann number *In the Bath*. Yvonne had the disgraceful idea of lugging six bathtubs into the studio. They were filled with hot water, Radox and foaming salts, and there we sat, warbling away while getting to work with the loofah. Well, if you've got to perform your ablutions in front of seven million people, you might as well enjoy it. Indeed, so pleasurable and relaxing did it become that we contrived somehow to get a large number of 'takes' slightly wrong, so that we would have to start all over again. By the time Yvonne declared herself satisfied we had been in the baths for an hour and a half. We emerged a little wrinkled but smelling divine.

October and November saw us back in the United States, touring this time for Columbia Artists rather than for Mariedi Anders. Our decision to change our American agent was sad but inevitable. Mariedi is a classical music specialist, and in that field she had done wonders for us considering the daunting problems of the market over there; moreover, she had handled us, and the sponsors who booked us through her, with unfailing charm and thoughtfulness. But, as we had done in Europe, we needed to break out of the classical music field and into the wider reaches of show business. And so, with much regret on both sides, we parted company with her organization.

The tour was the usual mixture of fun and hell. The latter was mostly to do with our itinerary, which involved driving ourselves about 7,500 miles in six weeks. Our ports of call were mainly medium-sized towns, but they also included New York City, Washington, D.C., and Boston. We reached the nadir at Sterling, Illinois. When we arrived at the hall for our rehearsal we discovered a group of wizened gents playing a fairly riotous game of shuffleboard on the floor in front of the stage. This, they told us, was a weekly fixture and they firmly declined to postpone it. After they left, our rehearsal was interrupted about every four minutes by a young lady who was using the auditorium as a short cut and carried a trannie playing heavy metal rock at full blast. For the concert in the evening the hall was half empty, and for the first time in our experience we were not asked for an encore. This lack of enthusiasm was explained (or so we like to think) when we arrived at a reception afterwards. None of the guests paid us the slightest attention: their eyes were glued to the World Series baseball on television.

We also had some bizarre experiences. Sandford, one of our five venues in North Carolina, is in the heart of the Bible Belt, where drinking in public is frowned upon. Our host here was Joe Peyt Stanton, a massive gentleman in size 15 boots and a lumberjack's cap. The post-concert party consisted of slugs of vodka furtively decanted from a bottle in the boot of Joe's rusty old Cadillac in the car park. A more formal dinner followed at a transport caff neaby, where we drank beers concealed in a brown paper bag. Then at Hershey (home of the immortal Hershey Bar and other confectionery) we noted with delight that our concert hall was by the intersection of Chocolate and Cocoa Avenues. Such a location, one might think, was a perfect spot to meet, as we did, a jolly group of matrons who were members of that august body, the Daughters of the British Empire. But even this curious conjunction ramified still further in hindsight: the Daughters were from the Harrisburg chapter; the nuclear power station at Three Mile Island that nearly bust a gut is only about a dozen miles down the road from Hershey. After that, it seemed perfectly natural that our reception following the concert at Troy (N.Y.) should be held in the local funeral parlour. Why it should have been held there we have no idea – it seemed tactless to ask. (Alastair: 'One of our Trojan hosts gave great delight in asking, "Where do you go from here – Ithaca?" ')

Still, in the big cities, and especially in Washington and Boston, we had large and enthusiastic audiences, and we began to feel that we were making headway. And at one of our New York City concerts, at the Cloisters Museum, we had the now very rare pleasure of presenting a concert devoted entirely to music of the fourteenth to sixteenth centuries.

II

No sooner were we beginning to recover from the jet lag and the general exhaustion of our American tour than we were off to Norway and Sweden for a formidable crowded week of concerts in Uppsala, Stockholm, Gothenburg, Oslo and Lund. The theatres were full and the audiences were friendly—and none was friendlier than that at Lund, our last port of call.

At the end of our concert there we were invited to a student house for a drink and a bite to eat. By this time we were pretty exhausted; moreover, at lunch-time on the following day four of us had an appointment at Cambridge University. So we stipulated that we would just drop in for a brief cordial for the sake of appearances, and then we would be on our way. And that, more or less, is what we did. We arrived at the hostel at 10 p.m., and left promptly at 5.15 a.m. (Nigel wishes it to be known that he was in bed by 2 a.m.) An extremely noisy party had got under way by the time we arrived. There was dancing, there was lots of lovely food, and there appeared to be a schnapps refinery in the kitchen. Every time our glasses were re-charged, a male-voice octet sang a different song in celebration—proving on that basis alone to have a very extensive repertoire. After this had been going on for some time the secret leaked out that our hosts were determined to see if we were made of the same stuff as Manhattan Transfer, whom they had entertained a couple of weeks previously and who had last been seen crawling into a sauna at 6.30 in the morning. Well, by about 5.00 in the morning we *were* made of the same stuff—we don't know its name but it was 95 proof. It was definitely time to go, we averred, nodding sagely at each other while someone filled our glasses again and the octet burst into song. Somehow we got out of the hostel, tumbled into the car of a volunteer chauffeur, and were driven to our hotel in Malmö about twenty miles south of Lund. It was at this point that we became aware of something missing, apart from our faculties. Where was Al?

We discovered later that he had risen to depart with the rest of us but that, fearing we might not have observed all the niceties in our leave-taking, had felt it incumbent upon him to shake everyone's hand several times, inspect the kitchen, read a meter or two, and in general satisfy himself that everything was proceeding in an orderly fashion. This proved to be thirsty work, but eventually he felt able to say goodbye. The hostel's self-locking front door closed behind him—but our car had departed. Aware that if he banged on the door he might be enrolled for a three-year course, possibly in the study of *vitis vinifera*, Al decided to walk. So it came about that several citizens of Lund were startled to be accosted at 5.30 in the morning by an English gentleman, dressed in immaculate camelhair coat and carrying a briefcase, who asked: 'Can you tell, my dear fellow, the way to Malmö?'

Eventually he managed to hitch a lift, and arrived at the hotel to find his colleagues helping each other to lift heavy objects (hankies, socks, etc.) into their suitcases. We were then conveyed to the airport. Al, Nigel, Simon and Brian managed to get to Cambridge in time for the annual dinner and concert for past choral scholars at King's.

III

The last three weeks before Christmas gave us no respite, with numerous concerts all over the country, another in Brussels, a couple of television recordings, and several radio broadcasts. One of the most enjoyable of these occasions was when we combined with the Richard Hickox Orchestra to give a Christmas concert at St. Margaret's, Westminster. The members of the orchestra are old friends of ours, and some of them were contemporaries of Al, Simon and Brian at Cambridge. Just to complete the circle we asked Sir David Willcocks, whom many of us had known as the distinguished organist at King's, to arrange some carols for our combined forces.

In terms of our future, the most significant event that Christmas time was the official announcement that Bill Ives was going to replace Alastair. It had been agreed that Alastair's last appearance with the group would be at our tenth anniversary concert the following May. Meanwhile, Bill had to give a term's notice to the college at Chichester where he was teaching, and snatch what free time he could to get acquainted with our repertoire in general and the tenor parts in particular. He turned up for his first rehearsal in the new year and astonished us with the amount of material he had already learnt by heart. It was comfortingly obvious that he was a 'natural' for the job. (Bill's version: 'Who else would take the job?')

We began 1978, once again, with a Scottish Arts Council tour, and followed this with our customary annual jamboree at the Queen Elizabeth Hall. Then we went over to Holland for our most ambitious engagement there so far. Our friends at Radio Vara had finally summoned up the nerve to book us into the legendary Concertgebouw in Amsterdam—and they were rewarded with a packed house.

A week in Italy (when Rome, you will recall, closed its door to us) and another in West Germany effectively took care of February. The results in Germany, especially, continued to be vastly encouraging. During a trip there in 1977 we had recorded enough material for two fifty-minute shows for the ZDF television company. Now, on this visit, we mimed the tracks on film, and the results formed the basis of two Sontagskonzerts that were televised throughout West Germany. Towards the end of

February a ZDF film unit came to England and spent six days filming each of us pursuing lives of blameless domesticity. (This gave Simon the chance to display his obsession with geriatric cars: part of his day before the cameras was spent driving his family around in his 1926 Austin 7—which, it is rumoured, the German audience took to be British Leyland's much heralded successor to the Mini.)

Just to prove that even German promoters can commit the most appalling musical bloomers, our concert in Hamburg during our February week almost turned into an action replay of the shambles at the Sistine Theatre. It was our first concert in this great city and the promoter, desperately anxious to fill the cavernous Musikhalle, had given away about 400 tickets to school children, apparently accompanying the gift with the suggestion that they were about to witness a combination of Abba and the Beatles. So of course our madrigals got the bird, and we were beginning to wonder if we were in danger of being mugged by a thousand teenie-boppers when our close-harmony set finally quietened them down. This time, however, there was a happy sequel. We earned an enormous picture and a vastly flattering article in *Die Zeit*, in which the writer apologised to us on behalf of the German public, begged us to return to Hamburg, and praised us to the skies.

Party-time in Hamburg, when we followed our concert in the Musikhalle with a party to meet the German press, organized by our German agent and the Head of our German record company (Erica Esslinger and Horst Schmolzi, both kneeling).

On Easter Monday, back in England, we broke our rule against interrupting our holidays at a cabaret evening at the London Hilton mounted by and for Datsun cars. We shared the bill with Ronnie Corbett and Mike Yarwood. Tony was in the process of losing his voice throughout the evening, and by the time we came on stage towards midnight the room was so thick with cigar smoke that the rest of us scarcely dared to take breath. The night was saved by Brian's setting of a Datsun repair manual to an Anglican chant.

We spent April in a not too strenuous tour around England and Wales, trying to pace ourselves for the anniversary concert. Bill came with us, joined in rehearsals, and generally got the feel of our methods of work. (He was struck chiefly by the enormous amount of time and energy we devoted to discussing such things as what colour of shirts we should wear.) One of the most pleasant of these tour concerts was at Ferndale, near Pontypridd, where we had been invited to perform to celebrate the fiftieth birthday of the local male-voice choir. Afterwards we repaired to an upstairs room of a pub run by two members of the choir. There was lots to drink and a great deal of talking, joking and friendly argument. Every now and then someone in one or other of the groups scattered about the large room would quietly begin to sing, and gradually other choir-members would take up the song until the whole place was a great wall of beautiful sound, with thirty or so more-than-tipsy Welshmen singing in perfect harmony.

So at last we came to 1 May 1978, the day of our tenth anniversary concert. This was to be the first time we had performed on our own at the Royal Festival Hall, and for the past few weeks we had been phoning the box office almost every day to discover whether anyone was coming to see us. On the great day we learnt that the concert was a sell-out. We looked forward to meeting our friends—all 3,000 of them!—and were intensely relieved that Nigel's voice, which had totally vanished

Our tenth birthday party.

Receiving Gold Discs from Sir John Read, the Chairman of EMI International, on the occasion of our tenth anniversary concert in the Royal Festival Hall on 1 May 1978.

the previous week, had happily come home again. During the morning we combined a rehearsal with sound-balance tests for EMI and the BBC, both of whom were to record the concert. This was followed by a press conference on the platform and a seemingly endless photo session. After a longish rest in the afternoon we were all set—bright as paint, and with legs curiously lacking in muscle tone.

The audience gave us a marvellous reception and the concert passed like a dream. At the end of the first half we were intercepted as we were about to leave the platform by Bill Cotton, Controller of BBC TV, who in turn introduced Sir John Read, Chairman of EMI International. After saying a few very flattering words about the King's Singers, Sir John presented each of us with a gold disc 'to celebrate ten record breaking years'. The concert ended with the sound of 3,000 voices singing 'Happy Birthday'—a quite devastating moment. This was, of course, also the occasion of Alastair's farewell to the group, so the evening was a heady mixture of triumph and sadness.

Within two weeks in the spring of 1980 our audiences included no less than four great opera singers – Dame Eva Turner at the Royal Festivel Hall, Reri Grist in Saarbrücken, Rita Streich in Mülheim and Anneliese Rothenberger in Hamburg with whom we appeared on German TV. She later joined in Brian's birthday celebrations.

And So . . .

Well, we had survived our first decade. To say that we were surprised would be to imply that we had planned our career from the outset—which, if you have stayed with the story so far, you will know is far from true. And so, having celebrated the birthday, we knuckled down again to the business of earning a living.

The first six months of 1979 might seem to follow a familiar pattern, with long visits to Holland, Germany, Australia and New Zealand, but the break with the pattern came with the first Japanese tour in June and July, in which we were all glad to experience something entirely new, and the start of what is obviously destined to be a rewarding relationship. The Land of the Rising Yen has certainly opened its doors to us, and we look to the future there with some excitement.

Bill's first year was to include moments which were unusual, even for the rest of us, and high on the list must be the invitation to appear in the Royal Variety Performance at the London Palladium. On that particular occasion, an all-English cast was brought together as a special tribute to the Queen Mother, and we were indeed very proud to be included, sandwiched as we were between Showaddywaddy and Gracie Fields!

Everything was the same; and yet, of course, with the arrival of Bill, everything was different, too. We symbolised the contradiction by ordering brand new sets of performing suits—in exactly the same style as the old. We pruned our repertoire drastically because, although it now numbered well over a thousand items, we regularly performed only a small fraction of them. Our new singer gave the group quite a different appearance—Alastair being fairly tall and Bill, well, not so fairly

tall (although when we did our next show with Ronnie Corbett, Bill suddenly assumed the physique of John Wayne).

The very first concert of the new set-up was, ironically, to be at Sherborne School, where Alastair Thompson was born and bred; and it went without a hitch. Bill had, naturally, seen us perform many times over the years—indeed he probably had as deep a grasp of what we had been trying to achieve as anyone, including the rest of us. He had applied himself vigorously to the business of absorbing our technique and the various idiosyncrasies of our stage 'act'. What *was* new to him, of course, was our almost permanently nomadic mode of life and the curious things that happen to us on our travels.

The rude awakening to his new way of life was not long delayed. Soon after he joined us we made our first visit to Hungary, where we gave a concert of fairly serious music before a crowded audience in the ballroom of the Budapest Hilton. The next day we were paid £300 each in Hungarian forints and told we must spend it before leaving the country. As we were due to check in at the airport in two hours, this presented something of a challenge. Apart from the sheer difficulty, for such ascetic chaps as us, of actually buying £300-worth of goodies, it was likely that our

ブライアン・ケイ
（バス）

アラステア・トムソン
（テナー）

アラステア・ヒューム
（カウンター・テナー）

サイモン・カーリングトン
（バリトン）

ナイジェル・ペリン
（カウンター・テナー）

アンソニー・ホルト
（バリトン）

We do have a breakfast menu from a Japanese hotel which offers 'sclambled egg'. However, they do make a better job of our language than we do of theirs!

Stout Hearted Men – an exercise in music and movement, with Dame Hilda, for a BBC TV programme in which Hinge and Bracket were our guests.

In Japan.

purchases would cost almost as much in excess baggage on the plane. As we staggered back to the hotel, each bearing a mountainous assortment of trophies, tat and Tokaj, Bill said, 'Any moment now I'm going to wake up and find myself in the middle of a lesson.'

Well, he didn't. In fact, he established himself so quickly, and so successfully, that we all began to re-think our theories about indispensability. What could have been very worrying and unsettling turned out to be refreshing and stimulating.

Even at the time that the proofs of this book were being read, Nigel announced his decision to join the ranks of retired King's Singers. Having had the experience, only two years earlier, of searching for an ideal replacement for Alastair, we were able to use a similar technique of asking around quietly to see if people could make any recommendations. Again there was a narrow choice, and again we were lucky in finding Jeremy Jackman, about whom some words appear at the end of the book in the 'Singers' section. If Bill was surprised to find that his first concert was in Sherborne, imagine how Jeremy must have felt when his first appearance as a King's Singer was in Potchefstroom, South Africa!

THE KING'S SINGERS

Nigel Perrin   Anthony Holt
Alastair Hume   Simon Carrington
Bill Ives   Brian Kay

1. ANIMAL, VEGETABLE or MINERAL?
A song cycle from Michael Flanders and Donald Swann   *arr. Gordon Langford*

Transport of Delight)	Vegetable and Mineral
The Slow Train)	with Animal connections
Rockall	No Vegetable, barely an Animal and no Mineral of Value
The Sloth	Animal
Wompom	Animal, Vegetable and Mineral miraculously merge

2. ENGLISH AND ITALIAN MADRIGALS OF THE SIXTEENTH CENTURY

Fire, fire my heart	*Thomas Morley*
The nightingale	*Thomas Weelkes*
Retire, my troubled soul	*John Ward*
Contrappunto bestiale alla mente	*Adriano Banchieri*
Chichilichi cucurucu	*Domenica da Nola*
Mascherata de cacciatori	*Giovanni Gastoldi*

3. LALELA ZULU (1977)   Music: Stanley Glasser
Words: Lewis Nkosi

Ilihubo	(Chant)
Mambabo!	(Wow!)
Lala Mntwana	(Sleep, child)
Uhambo Ngesitimela	(Train Journey)
Egoli	(Johannesburg)
Umdanso WaseGoli	(Jo'burg Dance)

(Commissioned for The King's Singers by The Halle Concert Society)

INTERVAL

4. FIVE PART-SONGS FROM THE GREEK ANTHOLOGY, op.45   *Edward Elgar*

Yea, cast me from heights of the mountains
Whether I find thee bright or fair
After many a dusty mile
It's Oh to be a wild wind
Feasting I watch

5. THREE SONGS (1973)   *Roger Hemingway*

The Echoing Green	(Blake)
The Cloth of Heaven	(Yeats)
The Fly	(Blake)

6. ARRANGEMENTS IN CLOSE HARMONY
The King's Singers always end their concerts with a group of pieces from this side of their repertoire, which might include anything from folksongs and spirituals, to standard songs and contemporary pop material.

It is interesting to compare the construction of one of our current programmes with one from our early days (see p 27).

Enchanting Majesty

1. It is our bounden / duty and / pleasure / /
   To recount some of the events in the life of Queen E / lizabeth, the / Queen / Mother. / /
   We shall commence with one of the most important e / vents in her / life / /
   On the fourth day of August in the year of nineteen / hundred / she was / born. / /

2. The youngest daughter of the fourteenth Earl of / Strathmore and / Kinghorn / /
   The Queen Mother was christened Lady Elizabeth, Angela, / Margue / rite Bowes /
   Lyon. / /
   On the twenty-sixth of April nineteen / twenty / six / /
   She married His Royal Highness the / Grand young / Duke of / York. / /

3. In 1937 she became Grand Master and Dame Grand Cross of the Royal Vic / torian /
   Order / /
   Also Lady of the Most Ancient and Most Noble / Order / of the / Thistle, / /
   Having one year earlier in nineteen / thirty / six / /
   Become a Lady of the most noble / Order / of the / Garter. / /

4. (Change chant) It is a well known fact that the members of our most illustrious and glorious
   / Royal / Family / /
   Have a wide var / iety of / pastimes and / hobbies / /
   Including music, polo, speeding, garden parties, / Terry / Wogan / /
   And the / racing and / riding of / horses. / /

5. King Henry the Eighth was noteworthy for his coll / ection of / wives / /
   Queen Elizabeth the Queen Mother's most time-consuming hobby would seem to be the coll
   / ecting of / honorary de / grees. / /
   These she holds at the Universities of / Oxford and / Cambridge / /
   Belfast, Manchester, Leeds, Liverpool, St. Andrews, Glasgow, Edinburgh, London, Keele,
   Sheffield, Dundee, Dalhousie, Cape Town, South Africa, Columbia, New York,
   Melbourne, Australia, Auckland, New Zealand, the University of the West Indies and /
   Hali fax, / Nova / Scotia / /

6. She has also been Chancellor of the Universities of / Dundee and / London / /
   And is Master of the Bench Middle Temple, and an honorary Freeperson of the Companies
   of Shipwrights, Grocers, Bakers, Musicians / and of / Merchant / Taylors. / /

   Mother, Grandmother, Greatgrandmother, to the Family to / end all / families, / /
   Her shining example of love and devotion to her family and people indicates why King
   Farouk was right in his famous prediction, when he said that by the end of this century
   only five Royal households would remain, and that these would be Hearts, Spades,
   Diamonds, Clubs and the / Glorious / House of / Windsor. / /

For our appearance at the Royal Variety Performance we decided to sing this chant, *Enchanting Majesty*, to the Queen Mother. As it was written by the side of a swimming pool in Santa Barbara, California, only one week before the show there was not enough time to check all the facts. Experts in English history will no doubt be quick to point out that the date of the Queen Mother's marriage is embarrassingly incorrect.

CHANT 1

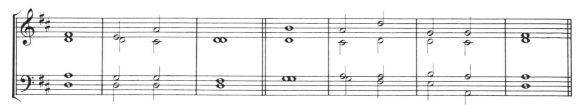

CHANT 2

The Music

The Music

The Sound

Ever since 1969 our line-up has consisted of two countertenors, one tenor, two baritones, and a bass. It is, in fact, a fairly common arrangement for the classical repertoire; removing, say, one of the countertenors and one of the baritones would thin the texture of the group sound; extra singers would be...well, too expensive, for one thing. In concert we usually include several pieces involving only four or even three members of the group so as to vary the tone.

Often, the two temporarily discarded singers will be the countertenors. This is for what Brian rather cheekily refers to as the 'men only' numbers, and it might be as well to settle the question of countertenors (or altos) first. This voice has, of course, a very long history. The present popularity of Handel's operas, and various modern works (notably by Benjamin Britten), have helped to restore the countertenor to classical music performance; while in the pop field the Beach Boys, Bee Gees, and other groups have made the countertenor familiar (if unrecognised as such) to millions of young listeners. Nevertheless, on the classical side, the terms 'countertenor' and 'castrato' were long held to be more or less synonymous; and in our earliest days both Nigel and Al had to get used to members of audiences coming up to them and whispering, 'D'you mind if I ask you rather a personal question?'

Most men have a falsetto 'head' voice in addition to their normal 'chest' voice. In physiological terms its production seems to depend on using only the 'edge' of the vocal chords; its effect can be likened to stopping a stringed instrument halfway up

All the excitement of the recording studio – cramped conditions, excessive amounts of hardware and no audience! As often as not Christmas carols must be recorded on the hottest summer day if they are to be processed in time for the festive season.

the fingerboard. A trained soprano can reach higher notes, and can also sustain for longer the highest notes in the countertenor's range; more significant, however, is the great difference in tone between the two voices. Individual countertenors vary considerably in range. Nigel is the 'top' voice in the group since he has a slightly higher range than Al. Likewise among our baritones: Tony has a higher voice than Simon's, enabling him on occasions to use the tenor range. These variations in range and tone, of course, contribute greatly to the richness of texture of our sound.

Many people have said that our particular sound is unique and unmistakeable. It is, at all events, something that we have worked at for many years. The aim has been to evolve a single six-voiced instrument. Just as six virtuoso fiddlers will not necessarily (indeed, will rarely) make a finely honed string ensemble, so six solo singers will not guarantee you a good vocal sextet. In each case the difficulty is not merely that soloists often lack extended experience of performing in a small group; the more intractable problem is that, however good each soloist may be, the particular sound he makes may not blend with the sound made by each of the other members of the group. Our sound is, first and foremost, the product of six highly compatible voices; but, over and above that, the combination of a perfect blend and of an individual group sound has been achieved by use of a variety of techniques —not all of which, it must be admitted, would have earned the approval of our singing teachers. (This question of vocal compatibility, incidentally, was one of the chief problems facing us when we had to find a successor to Alastair Thompson. Bill's tenor voice is, in fact, quite different from Alastair's, but both have one over-riding quality in common: they blend with the sound made by the rest of us.)

All good individual voices start with the God-given ability, actual or potential, to produce a beautiful singing tone. It is only after one has learnt how to harness one's physiological resources to produce such a sound that one can begin to tackle the quite different problem of expressing the sound in the form of words. Ultimately, of course, the ways in which one does this determine whether one is an artist or merely a goodish singer; but in any event, the marrying of sound and word is a technique that has to be acquired. Everyone has heard vocal performances in which the sounds are beautiful but leave one unmoved because one cannot 'hear' the lyrics. In a vocal sextet this potential danger is multiplied six times: each singer has his own particular way of speaking a word—but they must all sound the same when they sing it. Our early training as choir boys, when we were taught to 'spit out' the words with great clarity, has enabled us to defeat the problem of enunciation; our experience, especially in singing comic numbers whose effect depends on the listener instantly understanding every word, has helped us polish our technique. The same applies to our various 'special effects', as when we imitate the sounds of musical instruments or of animals.

Repertoire

As we have indicated in the journal, our repertoire has evolved partly as a result of our training as choral scholars and partly from the tradition at Cambridge of spare-time close-harmony singing. Although our range has expanded very considerably since our student days, the directions in which it has gone can in general be traced back to those two sources.

On the more serious musical side Simon, especially, has devoted countless hours to researching in specialist libraries for suitable material, such as madrigals, Renaissance motets, and much else. Apart from their suitability to the group's vocal resources, such pieces must be not only musically interesting but also accessible to audiences who may be unacquainted with the particular genre.

Even if, like Simon, you are familiar with any of the sources, this weeding out process is more difficult than it may sound. For instance, in the course of one of his researches he came across a madrigal collection by the sixteenth century Flemish composer Giaches de Wert. The collection ran to several volumes, and Simon picked his way through every single madrigal. Even after eliminating all the pieces that were outside the group's vocal range he still found himself with well over 100 potentially suitable madrigals. He played these through on the piano, and finally submitted a shortlist of about forty to the rest of us. We had a series of 'sing through' sessions to evaluate these, at the end of which only *one* madrigal found its way into our immediate repertoire. This may sound like a waste of Simon's time. In fact, the madrigal in question was Wert's beautiful setting of one of Petrarch's sonnets on the death of his beloved Laura, *Valle, che de lamenti miei*. It is one of the loveliest Renaissance works of any kind that we have found; it has been sung by us all over the world, and we included it on our English and Italian madrigal album.

As well as the individual ideas for repertoire which each of us may come up with, we have always enjoyed a wealth of suggestions made by interested parties outside the group. People who enjoy our work in a certain field regularly send copies of works which they think would suit us – we even had to go to Hungary to be introduced to one English madrigal, which we had previously overlooked!

One of our most rewarding ways of extending the repertoire has been to commission works, often from young composers yet to make a name for themselves. The brief given to a composer on such occasions is quite simple—the approximate length of work required, the range of each of our voices and the audience for whom the piece will be performed. Funds for such commissioning have come from a variety of sources, notably the Arts Council of Great Britain, the Performing Rights Society, and the Vaughan Williams Trust; commercial organizations such as the John Lewis Partnership have also made valuable contributions. The first work we commissioned was Sebastian Forbes's *Second Sequence of Carols*, which we performed with the Academy of St. Martin-in-the-Fields on our London début in 1968. Another piece that formed the backbone of many of our early concert programmes was the

Shortly after Bill joined us! In fact the climax of Paul Pattersons's *Time Piece* as recorded by German television.

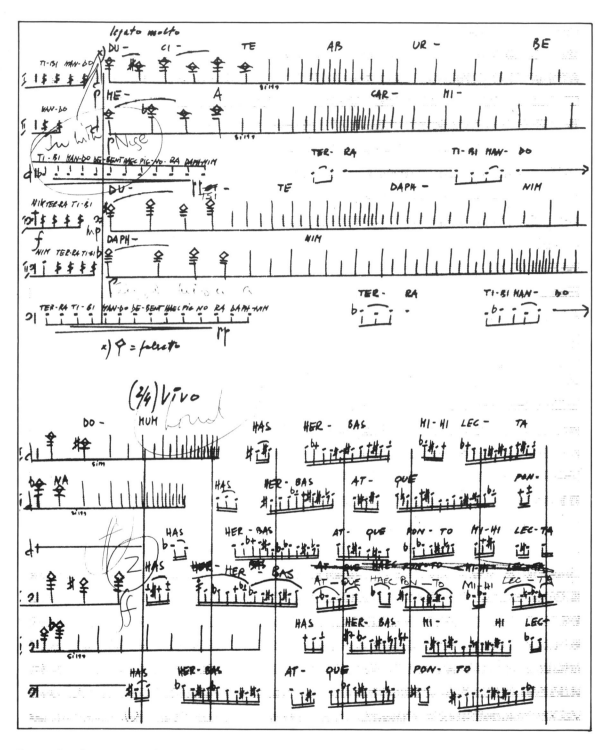

Part of *Ecloga VIII*, which the Polish composer, Penderecki, wrote for our appearance in the Edinburgh Festival of 1979.

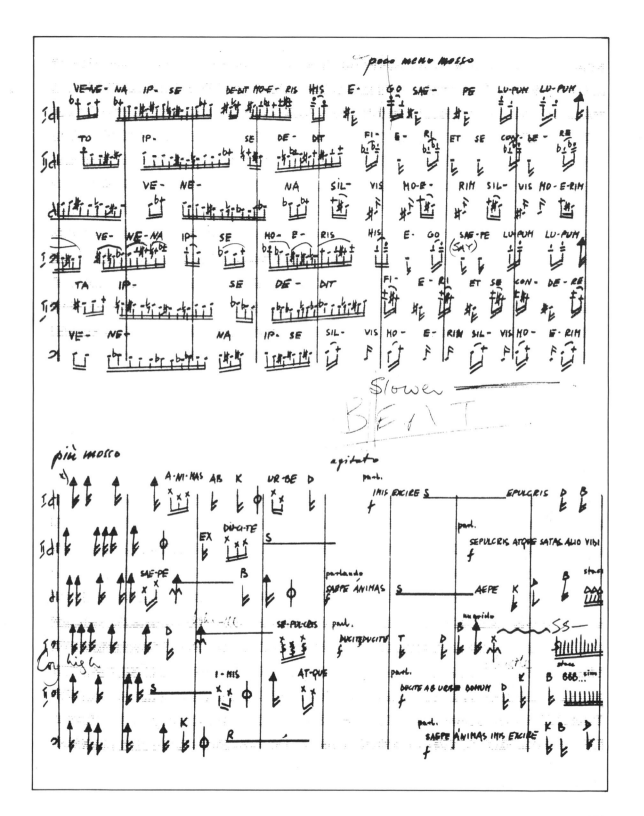

121

Wymondham Chants, commissioned from Geoffrey Poole, who at the time was a student at the University of East Anglia. Geoffrey Poole was, incidentally, introduced to us by Philip Ledger, the then Dean of Music at East Anglia, who later became Director of Music at King's College, Cambridge. This complex piece is made up of four contrasting movements, including some dramatic solos, and it helped greatly to establish our reputation for tackling work that is both musically difficult and yet appeals to a wide range of audiences.

The committees of some of the many festivals at which we have been invited to perform have also helped with commissions. Two internationally known composers, Krzysztof Penderecki and Luciano Berio, both wrote pieces for us at the invitation of the Edinburgh Festival committee. The Cheltenham Festival of 1974 commissioned an entire concert programme for us on the theme of the *Seven Deadly Sins*—each piece by a different composer. The result was an extraordinary but exhilarating mixture ranging from Anthony Gilbert's austere and spiky setting of Blake's *A Poisoned Tree* to Carl Davis and William Rushton's *Covetousness*, a hugely melodramatic Edwardian mini-operetta, later to become better known as *Sir Harry North's Last Case*.

The Camden Festival of 1973 commissioned what has long been one of the most popular and exciting items in our repertoire: Paul Patterson's *Time Piece*, which rests on the simple premise that all went well in the Garden of Eden until Adam took to wearing a wrist watch. In addition to its enormously skilful weaving together of many musical strands, from *avant-garde* to light music kitsch, the constant repetition of the phrase 'tick tock' has made the work readily understandable to all audiences. In spite of countless performances, *Time Piece* is so fascinatingly taxing a work to perform that it has never lost its freshness either for us or for our audiences.

The group's travels to many parts of the world have also resulted in a rich harvest of works by overseas composers. One of the most popular of recent years has been *Lalela Zulu*, with words by Lewis Nkosi and music by Stanley Glasser. The title means, roughly, 'listen to these Zulu sounds', and the work consists of six songs about the life of Zulus in Johannesburg. Another recently commissioned piece is *Mediterranean Suite* by the Maltese composer Charles Camilleri, which captures the flavour of the indigenous music of North Africa, Spain, Sicily, Malta, Greece, and Israel.

In the early 1970s we began what was to develop into an intensely rewarding and enjoyable relationship with Richard Rodney Bennett. For our annual Queen Elizabeth Hall concert in 1972 we gave the first performance of Richard's *The House of Sleepe*, settings from a sixteenth-century translation of Ovid's *Metamorphoses*. This work was commissioned by us with the help of a grant from the Arts Council. It is probably the most distinguished piece of music written for us so far. Although it is decidedly *avant-garde* in style and uses a form of 'time-space' notation, it has enraptured non-specialist audiences all over the world.

Arrangers

Richard Rodney Bennett provides a link with another major strand in our repertoire: the specially commissioned arrangements of every type of song from madrigals to pop. Richard's talent is almost unfairly wide-ranging, and he has also done a number of strikingly original arrangements of popular standards for us. These have included songs by Irving Berlin and Michel Legrand and, perhaps finest of all, a suite of five Gershwin songs; he is also responsible for the arrangement of one of our most enduringly popular individual numbers, Randy Newman's *Dayton, Ohio*.

We have been lucky enough to work with many other enormously accomplished arrangers over the years, including George Martin, Ron Goodwin, Jeremy Lubbock, Carl Davis, Joseph Horovitz, and (on many television spectaculars) Peter Knight. But two arrangers in particular have profoundly influenced not only our repertoire but also our style, especially in the light music field. The first, Gordon Langford, was one of our earliest regular arrangers and was responsible for many of the numbers on our first album, *By Appointment*. Apart from his rich resources of musical wit, Gordon has shown an unerring ability to exploit our sound to the full, and he has been responsible for countless beautiful arrangements of folk songs and popular ballads. His version of *The Peanut Vendor* was the most popular of our early close-harmony numbers (and enjoyed a brief revival at the time of President Carter's election), while his *Widdecombe Fair* remains one of our most often requested encores.

Daryl Runswick has become our most resourceful concert-programme arranger. A contemporary of Al, Simon and Brian's at Cambridge, Daryl originally worked for us as a bass-player on our 1973 George Martin album. But his arranging talents first exploded on the group with his version of the Lennon/McCartney *Obladi Oblada*. This is an authentic virtuoso piece. Since the Beatles made it a world-wide hit, its tune is familiar to most audiences. But Daryl added many extra ingredients, including snatches of Rossini overtures, Hollywood film schmaltz, Schumann's peasant dance, and much else. We view each new Runswick arrangement with a mixture of horror and exhilaration; but, once mastered, his pieces are usually breathtaking in both senses of the word. He has worked wonders with composers as diverse as Noel Coward, Hoagy Carmichael, and Gilbert and Sullivan—his *Patter-Matter*, a greased-lightning epitome of the best known G & S patter songs, being typical of his arrangements for us.

Another arranger who has provided us with a considerable number of delightfully idiosyncratic concert showpieces is David Overton (a Grimsby solicitor!). His work includes versions of Cole Porter songs to which he adds not only the odd line or two but also allusions to Bach and other unlikely collaborators. He has also furnished us with some cruelly witty parodies of contemporary pop numbers. As with the more serious side, several of our pop arrangements have simply appeared in the post from people we have never met, but who have rapidly been added to the list of available arrangers.

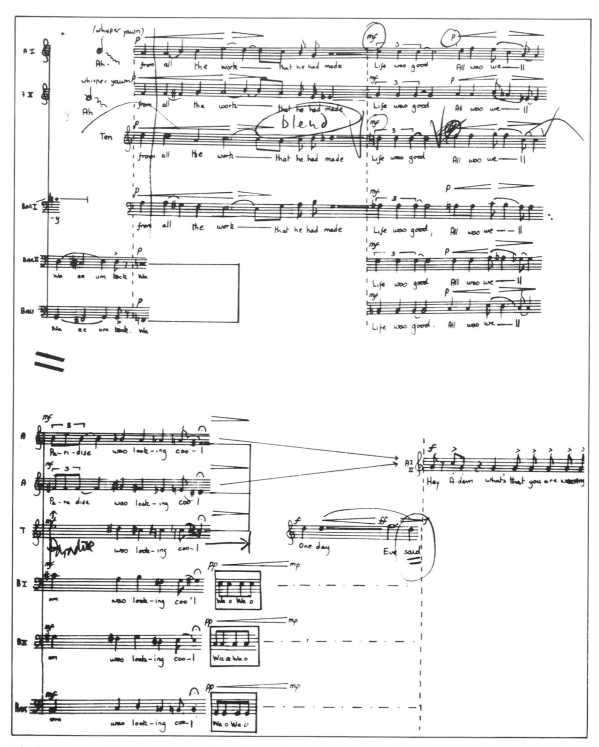

The beginning of Paul Patterson's *Time Piece* which was commissioned for us by the Camden Festival for our concert there in March 1973.

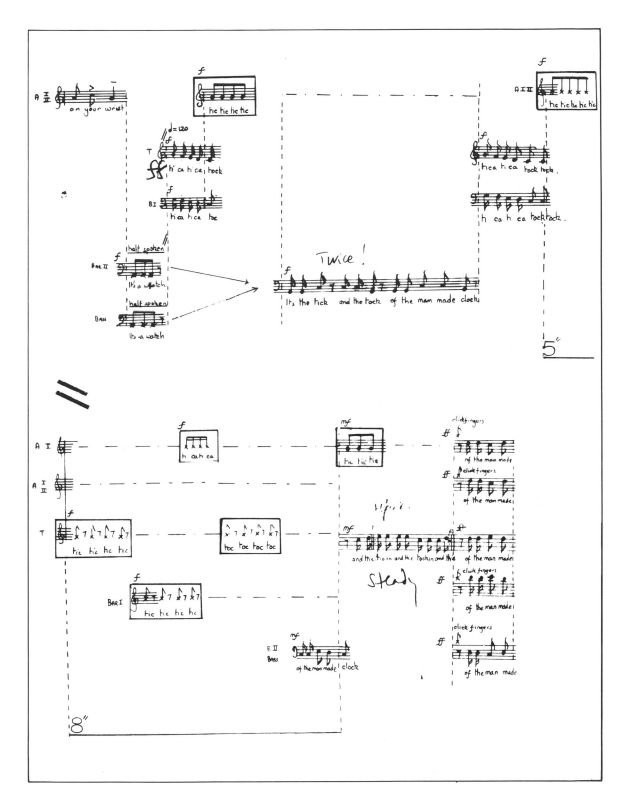

The Peanut Vendor, Gordon Langford's first close-harmony arrangement for us,
later orchestrated for a full dress rendition on Mantovani's BBC television show.

126

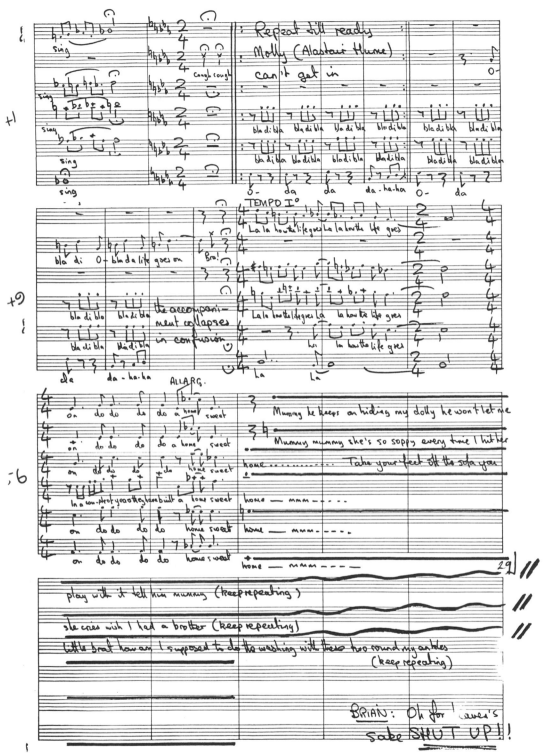

Part of Daryl Runswick's impeccable manuscript of *Obladi Oblada*, the sight
of which originally filled us with terror.

Preparation

Like many other busy musicians, we rarely enjoy the luxury of long periods for rehearsal – but, because we work together full time, we are able to bring new material gradually up to performance standard over a period of weeks or sometimes months. We can sight-read the majority of our new repertoire with reasonable accuracy, but there is a huge gulf between a heads-in-the-copy read-through and the final presentation to an audience or indeed a microphone. Unlike session singers, we never turn up to a studio recording unrehearsed and we are unhappy unless our concert material is all but memorised; the audience is as important to us as the music. Occasionally, we will ask an arranger or composer to help if we become bogged down or are uncertain of his intentions but, in general, we work alone.

Our practice has always been to sit together around a table, each of us listening like a hawk to three distinct elements: his own voice, the total sound of the group, and the sound made by each of the other five singers. The capacity to listen with 'three ears', each quite separate yet each providing feedback for the other two, takes some time to acquire – but it has proved an enormous help to us in fine-tuning our songs. Once we are confident technically we will launch a piece at an audience and use their response to help us with the final adjustments to timing or style. Sometimes an audience can point us towards an effect in the music which we have overlooked and sometimes lack of audience reaction can indicate with painful clarity an effect of which we are very proud – that would be best left out!

Some of our specially commissioned works, of course, have required much more rehearsal time than other of our pieces. *The House of Sleepe* was probably the most complicated and difficult of all so far and was, moreover, written in a form of notation with which we were unfamiliar. Although it is only about twelve minutes long, we spent a total of seventy hours rehearsal time on it before the first performance. Today we know the work pretty well; we would need to spend perhaps a few minutes rehearsing one or two passages before giving a concert performance.

The precision and fluency in performance which, we suppose, many people regard as our trade mark does not ingratiate us with everyone. A reviewer in the *Financial Times* in August 1976 lamented our 'supreme ability to reduce all the music (we) sing to its lowest common denominator'. The message seemed to be that we are too slick or too bland for that reviewer's taste. This is a problem in so far as it reflects on our efforts to deliver even the most complex songs apparently without difficulty. Some people have, in fact, urged us to introduce 'deliberate mistakes' occasionally in order to show audiences that many of our songs are hard to render perfectly.

This sounds to us like cheating. It's much better to enjoy one's authentic bloomers. On one occasion we sang Gordon Langford's appallingly elaborate version of *Widdecombe Fair* as an encore. We had not performed the piece for some time and, in the middle of it, Tony completely forgot his words. We all burst into helpless laughter, and the audience joined in—delighted to discover we are just as vulnerable to banana skins as anyone else.

Blow Away the Morning Dew, a close-harmony arrangement in Gordon Langford's hand, as it appears on the printed page. The notes are easy enough to read and learn quickly, but a lot of work is necessary on the sound of the chords, and on any 'business' which we may wish to add before it ever reaches the concert platform.

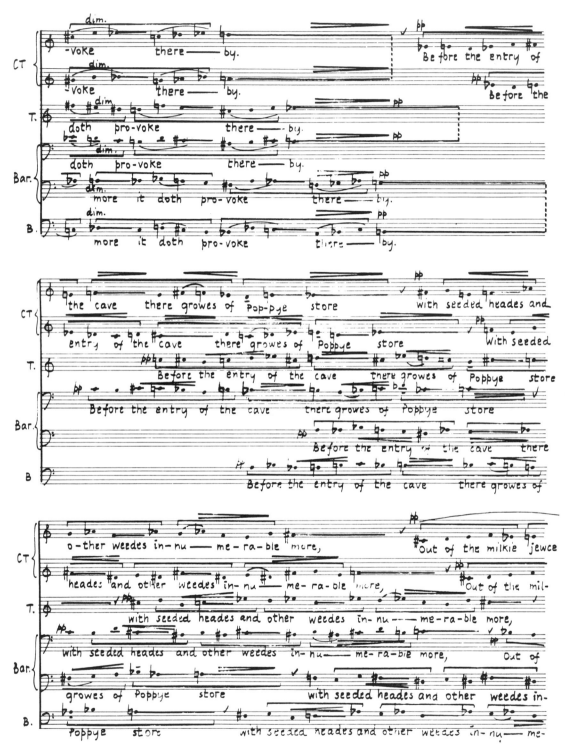

Part of Richard Rodney Bennett's superb hand-written score of *The House of Sleepe* which we commissioned in 1971.

Logistics

Our agent once wrote that a stranger who happened to surprise the King's Singers in conclave 'might well think that he had chanced upon a board of bankers contemplating charges, or a posse of lay preachers planning an assault on unholy places'. Leaving aside our always impeccable appearance and devout cast of countenance, we think we know what he meant. We do spend an inordinate amount of time discussing every conceivable aspect of our business as musical entertainers.

It was not always so. In the early days we would simply meet in one or other of our homes and work for a few hours on the programme for a specific concert; then we might have a brief chat to discover if all of us would be available for a subsequent concert, perhaps in a few months' time. Nowadays, planning involves complex problems in a whole variety of areas. If we are making a tour, travel arrangements must be planned to the last detail: whose cars we shall use, where we shall stay at the various venues (it's usually at hotels, but sometimes we stay with friends who happen to live in the neighbourhood); how we are going to find time for an early morning radio 'spot' that will undoubtedly help to boost the tour; how we are going to fit in sessions with the local press. At each venue we must allow ourselves two hours for an afternoon rehearsal. We spend only part of this time in going through the programme for the evening show; the rest is devoted to testing the acoustics (especially important in halls where we have not sung before) in order to determine the exact places—to within an inch or so—to position our music stands, checking the lighting in the hall and learning new music.

Programme planning also takes a great deal of time. Over the years we have performed countless concerts in almost every corner of Britain. Given our large and constantly growing repertoire, it is not difficult to avoid singing the same songs in the same place twice. But in order to make certain, we still have to check through anything up to ten or twenty old concert programmes to discover exactly what we *did* sing at a certain venue and at other halls in what might be termed the same catchment area. Another difficulty in planning programmes arises when we commit ourselves to an engagement in the distant future (many of our concerts are booked two and even three years ahead). We know that, by the time such engagements come round, we shall have added considerably to our present repertoire; on the other hand, the festival committees or concert-series promoters who have invited us to these far-ahead engagements, need to print their programmes many months in advance of the event.

Much of our working lives is devoted to performances on the concert platform. On our highly concentrated (and often exhausting) overseas tours we never give more than five concerts in a week—nine in a fortnight is the preferred maximum—and seldom perform more than three nights in succession. Our British tours usually have a less hectic itinerary nowadays—but we tend to be involved in other activities at the same time. We spend many hours in the recording studio (we make at least three albums every year); we are frequently rehearsing and then recording television and radio shows; we are involved in press and television interviews; and then there are such things as publicity photo sessions, checking proofs of printed programmes for forthcoming tours or individual concerts.

This last brings us to the constantly recurring problem of what we are going to wear at a concert or television show. We have several performing suits and a staggering collection of different coloured shirts. These, too, are the subject of protracted and sometimes quite heated discussions as to suitability for particular occasions.

All these questions—whether or not to accept an engagement, the development of programmes for specific shows, the acceptance or rejection of new items for the repertoire, travel arrangements, what to wear, and much else—take so long to resolve because they are decided democratically, on a show of hands, after each of us has had the opportunity to state his point of view. No doubt it would all be much simpler if we appointed a *Gauleiter*, who would make instant decisions and issue directives. We do not, however, care for *Gauleiters*.

Filming in London for the BBC TV programme *That's Life* – one occasion on which we didn't need much help from the wardrobe department!
In the words of Peter Christie:
For we're the nouveau poor
The wolf is at our door.
We're in Burke's Peerage, we're in Who's Who,
We're in the red and penury too;
But that's non-U no more,
For we're the nouveau poor!
(An Instant Sunshine song, which we included on our album *New Day*)

A Victorian collection, recorded for BBC television as part of *Century of Song.*

Ballads, Songs and Snatches – a tele-recording of Daryl Runswick's conglomeration of Gilbert and Sullivan patter songs.

The Singers

The Singers

Nigel Perrin

Nigel joined the choir of his local church at the age of seven, and has clear memories of his very first service there. When his mother asked him what he had sung, he explained that the longest and trickiest piece was something called *Magnifying the Cat*. At this time his father was an officer in the RAF and was subject to frequent postings to stations in England and abroad. If Nigel were to receive an uninterrupted education it was clear that he would have to go to a boarding school—preferably one at which his liking for music would be encouraged. And so in 1956, at the age of eight, he began his formal singing career as a choristere at Ely Cathedral, where he was to stay for ten years. He was lucky in that, when his voice broke at the age of thirteen and a half, he did not have to wait months for it to settle: for musical purposes it merely dropped a bit,

Nigel, with trombone, as a joyful winner in the Hill House music competition, 1965.

and he made a swift transition from treble to alto, which is what he has been singing ever since.

In the senior school at Ely he lit no academic bonfires. His chief interests outside music were sport and theatricals. Much of his most enjoyable music-making at this time was with the school's Madrigal Society, which was founded by one of the masters, Roger Firkins (an ex-King's choral scholar). The society was demanding musically but delightfully informal socially. It became even more popular when recruits were enrolled from Ely High School for Girls—who not only increased the repertoire but, more important, had to be escorted to the bus station after rehearsals. Nigel took to playing the trumpet and later the bass trombone and honked away in the school band.

In September 1965 he attended the alto trial at King's College, Cambridge, was awarded a scholarship, and went up the following year. Unlike his predecessors, Al, Simon and Brian, he took no part in the activities of the Footlights Club; much of his spare time was devoted to girlfriends or sport. Cricket was not permissible because matches invariably finished too late for choir practice. But Sir David Willcocks encouraged scholars to play rugby so long as they could furnish clear proof of having taken a shower before evensong.

Nigel left Cambridge in 1969 with a degree in history, English and theology. He moved to London (where he shared Alastair Thompson's flat) to take a Dip. Ed. course at King's College, London. The course convinced him he would not make a teacher, so he joined the choir of St. Clement Dane's in the City, and began also to sing as a freelance with many of the leading professional choirs. Since leaving Cambridge he had also sung from time to time with the Scholars and the King's Singers.

In September 1970, by now married, Nigel became a lay clerk at St. George's Chapel, Windsor Castle—a post which went with a house in the Cloisters. (When, after committing a parking offence in Nottingham, he was asked to give his address and said 'Windsor Castle', he got a very old-fashioned look from a constable and it was touch and go whether he would be hauled off to the police station for mocking the arm of the law.)

It was possible for some months to combine his lay clerk's work with an engagement with either the King's Singers or the Scholars on his one day off a week. He thought any problem of time off would be relieved when he decided to give up his work with the Scholars. As it turned out, of course, the King's Singers' engagement diary was steadily getting fuller and fuller at this time, and eventually his concerts with the group were taking up three or four days a week.

In some ways Nigel was a reluctant recruit to full-time singing: he had long held the

L to R: Barbara, holding Lorna, Victoria and Nigel with Abigail.

view that to devote one's life to earning a living as a musician would take the joy out of singing. The centre of his life is still very obviously his wife, his three daughters, and his circle of close friends. He likes nothing better than to relax in front of his log fire at home.

On their acre of land near Bath he digs the garden, chops wood, repairs and improves their large and ancient house, encourages the chickens to accomplish yet greater feats of productivity, prunes the fruit trees—and dreams his dreams of self-sufficiency.

Alastair Hume

Al's father was a natural, though untrained, musician—one of those enviable people who can hear a tune but once and, without benefit of sheet music, play it effortlessly on a piano. His mother had been a dancer with Sadler's Wells and was also a gifted singer. Together his parents wrote the book, lyrics, and music of no less than four full-scale pantomimes and produced them in the village hall.

Al claims that the sound of his sister shrieking about the house when they were young made him resolve never to have anything to do with singers or singing. In fact, his sister was trained at LAMDA, was a very fine soprano, and might have made a successful soloist had she not abandoned her career in favour of marriage. Still, it's true to say that Al was a late-comer to serious music-making. It was only in his third year

at Tonbridge School that he thought he might as well join the choir. He tipped a few bass-baritone staves at the choir master, who looked a little pained and asked him if he had tried alto. Al did not know what alto was, but the master demonstrated, Al imitated him—and was promptly signed on. He enjoyed the choral work, and in 1961 he was encouraged to take the alto trial at King's College. He failed that year, but he was accepted the next, for the 1962 intake.

Meanwhile, in much the same spirit, he had taken to learning the double-bass—with such success that he was accepted by the National Youth Orchestra. When he left Tonbridge in the summer of 1961, he went on tour with the orchestra to the Soviet Union and elsewhere. The orchestra was enormous, and Al vividly recalls the days that were spent at rehearsals at a school in Yorkshire. On one occasion each section of the orchestra practised by itself, and the sound of no less than 10 double-basses, not all of them perfectly tuned, sawing away in a rather small room had only to be heard to be disbelieved.

Having had two lessons and having actually worked out how to hold the thing, looking every inch the budding professional.

Cambridge University Squash Rackets Team.
1964 1965

R. D. B. Cooper
Trinity

H. R. Angus
St. John's

T. W. D. Hendry
Queens'

D. J. Cook
Caius

A. J. Hume
King's
(Captain)

S. R. G. White
Corpus

At King's College all did not run smoothly. On one occasion the great Sir David Willcocks told Al, 'You are without question the worst alto we have ever had in the choir.' Al needed no further encouragement: he worked like mad at his law studies (he was to emerge with a good degree in this subject). He also spent much time playing squash. He had played for Tonbridge, got his squash blue in his second year, and captained Cambridge in his third; he was later to play for both Sussex and Lancashire. Finally, of course, he was much involved with Simon and Brian in informal music-making.

On leaving Cambridge in 1965 Al joined the Cathedral Choir School at Chichester, and the following year was appointed a lay clerk, thereby becoming a colleague of Tony Holt's. In 1967 he had an audition with the BBC Northern Symphony Orchestra: he attributes its successful outcome to the fact that the conductor, George Hurst, was a lover of fine sports cars and was impressed with Al's formidable Jensen. Be that as it may, he played with the orchestra for three years. Then, in 1970, he moved from Manchester to London, joined the choir at St. Pauls's Cathedral, played with most of the major symphony orchestras in the

The Lagonda back on the road after a complete rebuild which took eleven years. Always 'about to be on the road in the summer', the summer was never specified.

capital—and somehow contrived to devote more and more time to the King's Singers. This multi-faceted career could not last, however, and when the group finally became full-time professionals, Al was delighted to throw in his lot with them—although even to this day he is occasionally visited by the conviction that by now he could have had a blamelessly comfortable solicitor's practice in some pleasant country town.

Al's artistic interests include music of all kinds and the theatre. He entertains a passion for old and beautiful objects—buildings, antiques of every kind, and especially old clocks and pipes. In much the same vein, he has a reckless enthusiasm for ancient cars and takes a special pride in his 1932 Lagonda 16/80 Special (although he is also to be discovered sneaking around the countryside in a middle-aged, but distinctly post-war, Bentley S.2). Open air sports continue to keep him impressively fit: he plays all racquet games with competitive fire, and he goes sailing whenever he has the chance. When there is no time for these, he will play you at backgammon (no cheques, please). As the best possible antidote to the 'fast foods' he is obliged to ingest on tours, he has opened a restaurant in a fourteenth-century barn in rural Somerset. On the rare occasions on which he has time to visit it, he assumes the guise of wine waiter.

Bill Ives

Bill grew up in the town of Diss, in Norfolk, and in 1956 at the age of eight, he became a fellow chorister of Nigel's at Ely Cathedral. He enjoyed the singing and his piano lessons, but within a few years became especially absorbed in composition. In those early days his playing of his own pieces tended more towards enthusiasm than artistry, and he recalls many occasions when his house master stole up behind him and bellowed: 'Don't thump, Ives!'

Although Bill was to join the King's Singers only in 1978, his connections with future members of the group, apart from Nigel, began in 1965. That year a group of choral scholars, including Brian and Simon, visited Ely to listen to the school's Madrigal Society summer concert. One of the pieces performed was Bill's setting of Edward Lear's *Calico Pie*. Simon and Brian liked the piece, took it away with them, and the following year it was included on the *Songs of Love* album.

During his final year at Ely there was to be a performance of Benjamin Britten's *War Requiem* at the cathedral, conducted by the composer. Bill collected together a bundle of his compositions and, summoning up his courage, approached Britten during a lull in rehearsals of the requiem and asked him to look at his work. Britten later wrote him an enormously encouraging letter.

In 1966 Bill was awarded a choral exhibition to Selwyn College, Cambridge. During his third year there he drove up to London every fortnight to study composition under Richard Rodney Bennett, whose enormous skill and versatility he had long admired—and whose works and arrangements Bill was, of course, later to perform with the King's Singers.

Summer 1949.

142

On leaving Cambridge in 1971, Bill joined Guildford Cathedral Choir, then under Barry Rose, who was later to become choirmaster at St. Paul's Cathedral. Bill managed to combine his choral work with teaching music at a school in nearby Cobham. With Rose's enthusiastic support he composed many pieces for the choir. Bill also took advantage of the many opportunities to conduct, and during the period 1971-6 he was, in fact, conductor at the annual Festival of Church Music at Edington, Wiltshire.

In 1976 he took a post as lecturer of music at Chichester College of Further Education, and for a time his singing was confined to weekly sessions with local chamber groups. The following year, however, brought three major milestones in his career. The first, owing much to Barry Rose's good offices, was an invitation to write an organ march for the Queen's Silver Jubilee Thanksgiving service at St. Paul's Cathedral. The second was to write and arrange a 45-minute Whitsuntide anthology which was broadcast by the BBC Singers. Finally, late one evening towards the end of June, he received a

Bill, aged 13, as a budding Liberace.

Ely Cathedral Choir in the early Sixties with Bill third from left in the middle row and Nigel on his left.

143

telephone call. It was Nigel ringing to enquire if Bill might be interested in filling the King's Singers tenor spot that was shortly to be vacated by Alastair Thompson.

'I had,' Bill recalls, 'followed the group's career closely since they started. I greatly admired not only their superb musicianship and confident interpretations in many different genres, but also their adventurous commissioning of work from serious modern composers. I envied what I took to be their glamorous life-style—dashing around the world and playing to packed houses. As for their invitation to me: it was fantastic—but they had to be crazy!' Crazy or not, he accepted the offer, and handed in his notice at Chichester. His first concert for the group was at Sherborne School—where he had attended a King's Singers concert some twelve years before.

Bill's life outside the group is spent at home in Sussex with his wife and young daughter. He is, he confesses, very much a home lover. After touring he likes nothing better than to potter about his garden, although he has been known to point an electric drill in the direction of a wall in the cause of do-it-yourselfery. His taste in music is rooted most deeply in the late nineteenth and twentieth centuries—he particularly admires Richard Strauss, Elgar, Debussy, Ravel, Stravinsky, Walton, Berg and Tippett. He devotes as much as possible of his spare time to composing, listing among his pieces a commissioned 25-minute work for four soloists, chorus, string orchestra, and organ.

On the concert platform, Bill is third from the left, between Al and Tony. In spite of his refusal to wear built-up shoes, he towers over his music stand.

With Beth at Charlotte's christening on Christmas Day, 1977. Nicholas Rhys Ives was born on 17 May 1980 while Bill was in Bayreuth and while the book was with the printer.

Tony Holt

Tony was born into a family of amateur music makers: his mother was a gifted solo singer, and his father and brother were members of the local church choir. One of his earliest musical memories is of singing rounds with his mother and brother while doing the washing-up at the kitchen sink. (One of the rounds was *Great Tom is Cast*, about the bell in Tom Tower at Christ Church, Oxford, which Tony would later know well.)

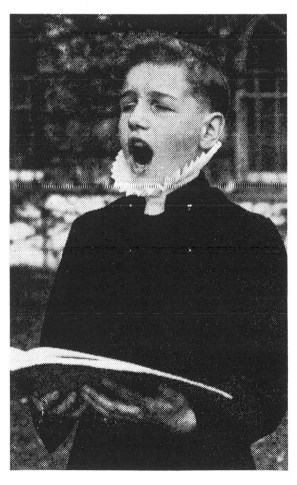

Tuning up for the Queen's Coronation in May 1953.

His first formal musical training was in the choir of his church at Barkingside, Essex. Tony showed early promise, and was sent on several Royal School of Church Music instructional course. He learnt the rudiments of notation as well as how to sing, how to breathe—and how to behave himself away from home. At the same time he began, reluctantly, to take piano and violin lessons. Although he loved singing he was scarcely a dedicated musician at this stage: at school he was more interested in sport. In the holidays he worked at the traditional boyhood pastime of 'mucking about'.

In 1955, at the age of twelve, he was one of twenty boys selected to represent the RSCM choir at the Coronation of Queen Elizabeth at Westminster Abbey. The boys were packed off for a month's intensive training at the RSCM's headquarters at Addington Palace—but five minutes from where he now lives. Here Tony spent the mornings on musical work, and in the after-

Summer 1962 in Arezzo with the Collegium Musicum Oxoniense, a little the worse for wear after a competition success.

noons he earned a bob or two as a caddy at the golf club next door. His mementoes of the coronation service are a medal, a coronation stool, and Vaughan Williams's autograph.

Soon afterwards his family moved to Clayton, on the Sussex Downs, and Tony went to Brighton College. He sang as a treble in the school choir for a while, then had to endure a long period while his voice turned first into a cracked alto, then into a cracked tenor, and finally arrived at a rather vague approximation of a baritone. These vocal fluctuations enabled him to devote more time to sport; but they did not save him from the displeasure of his violin teacher (an

Italian lady of unexampled ferocity) on the occasions when he opted out of lessons.

When his voice finally settled down Tony began taking private singing lessons, and at the age of seventeen (a year earlier than necessary) he went for the baritone 'trial' at King's College, Cambridge. The experience for him, 'a green youth from a seaside town', was daunting. The beautiful but austere room at King's, the panel of formidable-looking judges, including the celebrated Boris Ord, and the tense atmosphere made all his crotchets quaver! He failed the trial and, still smarting from the occasion, he tried his luck at Christ Church, Oxford. With great trepidation he knocked on the door at the appointed hour, to be greeted by the warm and avuncular figure of Dr Sydney Watson. The audition made a stark contrast to Tony's experience at King's. The matter at hand was broached only after ten minutes of friendly and relaxing conversation, by which time he had become convinced that the occasion was not so much a test as a *matinée musicale* to be enjoyed by both of them. Tony was awarded a choral exhibition; his headmaster congratulated him with a characteristic 'Well played, Holt!'

Before going up to Oxford, Tony joined the Tudor Singers, a Brighton choral group directed by Brian Judge, which was greatly to influence his musical education and outlook. The group consisted mainly of countertenors, tenors and basses from Oxbridge, plus a sprinkling of local sopranos. (Alastair Thompson sang with the choir on many occasions, while Simon and Al Hume put in appearances now and again.) The choir performed not only in Brighton but in London and abroad—and it was at a party after a concert in Norway that Tony became engaged to his future wife, a soprano in the choir.

Tony was to discover that the atmosphere created at his audition was a true reflection of Sydney Watson's attitude to choral work at Christ Church. The aim was, obviously, to make beautiful music and to engender a true appreciation of its worth. But there was no feeling that one had to strive for technical perfection at all costs; the emphasis was rather on the integral role the choir played in worship in the divine service. In part, of course, this emphasis derived from the fact that the chapel at Christ Church is also the cathedral of Oxford.

The chapel's position in the religious life of Oxford meant that Tony and his five contemporaries had a mixed reception at first from the lay clerks (the professional choir singers at Christ Church), many of whom had been there for some years. The position of choral exhibitioner had been recently created and the permanent staff, as it were, tended to regard with suspicion the young upstarts who sang in the choir only during term time. But gradually the barriers came down and harmony prevailed. On the other hand it is true that the exhibitioners did not 'live' choral music quite so intensely as the scholars at King's. For many of them the academic call was stronger than the vocal. For Tony music undoubtedly came first, but much of it was made outside the chapel choir. There were concerts with college music societies, operas (one a week!) with the opera club, and singing with a number of small groups, notably the Collegium Musicum Oxoniense directed by Laszlo Heltay. His experience of performing publicly in such a wide variety of music and situations was to be of enormous value to him when he joined the King's Singers.

Life at Christ Church mined a deep vein of eccentricity in the person of the Dean, Cuthbert Simpson, a man whose devoutness of character was matched by his earthiness of expression. In chapel the Dean's voice had to be amplified during eucharist, and on one famous occasion an organ scholar (obviously new to the job) gave him too high a note with which to intone the responses. The congregation sat astonished when, over the sound system, came the furious whisper, 'What does he think I am—a bloody canary?'

Having been awarded a degree that he describes, a little enigmatically, as truly reflecting the amount of work he had put in at Oxford, Tony got married and took a position as a lay clerk at Chichester Cathedral and teacher at the Choir School, which involved teaching prep-school boys as well as singing in the choir. In 1969, having

With wife, Janette, and children Sarah and Julian.

had his fill of teaching, he applied for a job as a baritone with the BBC Chorus, and went to work for the princely sum of £29 19s 8d per week (less tax). The chorus consisted of 28 singers, each a potential soloist, and the work was extremely challenging. Never-theless, he still found time to fulfil the occasional engagement with the King's Singers. Finally, when Richard Salter (with whom Tony had been at school in Brighton) left the group, Tony resigned from the BBC and joined the King's Singers full time.

Tony now lives in Croydon with his wife and teenage daughter and son. He has a very wide range of interests—notably art (especially the French Impressionists) and literature of all ages and genres; in music his record collection leans towards Italian Romantic opera and the works of Mozart and Richard Strauss. His old enthusiasm for cricket and soccer is now pursued from a sedentary position; disdaining the siren song of his more or less local Crystal Palace, he continues his lifelong support of Tottenham Hotspur. A member of the National Trust and the Royal Society for the Protection of Birds, he is strong in the cause of conservation and loves exploring the countryside. The recent onset of grey hair has galvanised him into jogging; his attempts to shame the other members of the group into joining him in tracksuits has met with only moderate success.

Simon Carrington

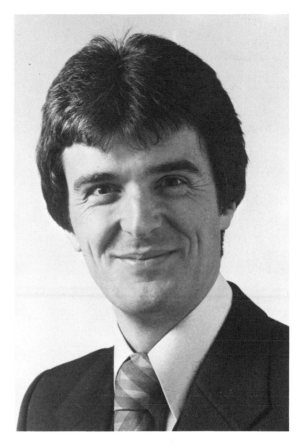

There was never much doubt that Simon was destined for a career in music. His father had been a choral scholar at King's College. His mother, who studied cello with Emanuel Feuermann, gave recitals at the Wigmore Hall with Gerald Moore until the war interrupted her career. (She now teaches and is President of the Music Masters' Association and an examiner for the Associated Board.)

At the age of seven, Simon attended chorister trials at Christ Church, Oxford and—in spite of suffering from a violent bout of 'flu and consequently being swathed from head to foot in a blanket—he impressed the choirmaster sufficiently to secure a place. In a sense his professional career begins at that point: the life of a young chorister at Christ Church Cathedral School involved disciplines that are normally expected only of adult musicians. On the other hand, the occasional perks were greatly to the liking of this particular eight-year-old, and Simon remembers with affection the canon's splendid tea-parties at Christmastime, and the fiercely contested games of bowls on the Dean's lawn after early morning service on saints' days.

When he was thirteen years old, Simon moved on to King's School, Canterbury, a school whose long musical traditions were now in the formidable hands of Edred Wright, an outstandingly gifted choir trainer. It was here that Simon finally acknowledged defeat at the hands of the cello and resorted to the double-bass. This was to prove a wise decision: he almost immediately gained a place as eighth bass in the National Youth Orchestra. On his first NYO course, at Portsmouth in 1961, he was to meet another rising bass-player, Al Hume.

That year he followed in his father's footsteps, becoming a choral scholar at King's College, Cambridge. He was to spend four years at King's. Like other founder members of the King's Singers, he blended the disciplined but intensely satisfying life of a choral scholar with a wide-ranging collection of fringe activities at the Footlights Club and elsewhere. In 1965 the Choir Eight for the May Races (held, it goes without saying, in June) included the enthusiastically crab-catching oars of Simon, Al, Brian and Alastair Thompson. At Simon's suggestion the boat was named after a Thomas Tallis canon. The tempo of this piece, the last of a

All those long hours of practice – for this?

London Palladium, here I come. Christ
Church Cathedral choir school some time in
the Fifties.

The first of a long line of ageing dependents.

150

With wife, Hilary, and Rebecca and Jamie.

series of eight hymn tunes, was defined by the composer thus: 'The eyghte goeth mild: in modest pace'. The boat's pace was certainly modest, but the *tempo* was less *largo* than *furioso*.

Bass-playing also took up much of Simon's spare time; he performed with many ensembles, and also developed a double double-bass 'act' with Al that was to be featured in the intervals at early King's Singers concerts.

In 1965 Simon went to New College, Oxford, for a year to study for his Diploma in Education. Here he continued to devote much of his time to making music—formally with New College choir, and informally with a variety of ensembles. As a result he made something of a breakthrough, if he did not actually set a precedent, by failing his Dip. Ed. exams. So he decided the double-bass was a likelier meal-ticket than teaching, and gained the appointment of sub-principal double-bassist in the BBC Northern Symphony Orchestra in Manchester. It was here that he met his future wife, who was a graduate of the Royal Manchester College of Music (she continues to teach piano to this day). Simon left the BBC Northern Symphony in 1967 and moved to Surrey, playing with most of the leading symphony orchestras in London while helping to launch the King's Singers.

Simon, his wife, and their daughter and son live in the Vale of Pewsey in Wiltshire with their two aged dependants—a 1926 Austin 7 and a 1927 Humber 9/20, both of which are remarkable sprightly although they rely on Simon's gift for mechanical prosthetics. Hyperactive by temperament, Simon somehow finds time between his King's Singers engagements to help both his children in their music studies, to dig the garden, to play with local amateur music groups, to restore his new home, to give succour to the Austin and the Humber, to research new items for the King's Singers repertoire; and he is in fearful peril of acquiring Tony's penchant for jogging. Every now and then his family prevail upon him, by main force if necessary, to sit in an armchair with a pipe in his mouth and a novel by Trollope in his hand—and such periods of relaxation often last for upwards of five minutes. Favourite family pursuits are walking in the countryside and taking narrow-boat holidays on the English canals. Simon also spends two weeks every August directing a choir at the Berwang Holiday Music Course in Austria.

Brian Kay

As children Brian, his sister and his two brothers assembled perhaps the largest collection of Brownie 127 cameras in Western Europe. No infant David Baileys they: the hardware was trophies they won, year in, year out, at talent contests at Scarborough, where they spent their summer holidays at their uncle's hotel. Brian's family has been steeped in music-making, both sacred and secular, for generations. He comes from a long line of Methodists (his great-grandfather was President of the Methodist Conference), and the tradition of singing out joyously and unashamedly in chapel was carried over into the home.

Music in chapel and parlour, and the experience of performing in public at Scarborough, bore rich fruit in Brian's generation: his younger brother Graham became a choral scholar at St. John's College, Cambridge, while his sister Heather ended up as one of the Swingle Singers; his older brother Barry is an enthusiastic opera singer, but has retained his amateur status. Brian went to Rydal School in North Wales, where his talent as a treble was recognised by the director of music Percy Heywood, who had been a choral scholar at King's. Here, too, Brian acquired further experience of singing in public: he and other members of the school choir performed at concert parties on the end of Llandudno pier and elsewhere on many occasions.

At school he was encouraged to concentrate on music from the age of twelve. But his voice stubbornly refused to break for over four years (he blames this entirely on an excessive intake of free school milk), and it was quite late in his Rydal days that Percy Heywood suggested he might have a stab at a King's College choral scholarship. To his delight and astonishment, he came top of the list for the 1963 intake of choral scholars.

Among his contemporaries at King's and elsewhere Brian particularly remembers the conductors Andrew Davis (who was to play the organ at Brian's wedding) and David Atherton, the early-music specialists David Munrow and Christopher Hogwood, the organist Simon Preston, and the tenor Robert Tear. As an active member of the Footlights Club he rubbed shoulders with such as John Cleese and Eric Idle, Clive James, Germaine Greer, and Daryl Runswick (who is now one of the King's Singers most valued collaborators in the field of musical arrangements).

Like many other choral scholars, Brian followed his three years at Cambridge with a

Only Father, who initially inspired us all to sing, is missing from the Kay Family Singers – Barry, Mother, Brian, Heather and Graham.

year's study at Oxford for a Diploma in Education. Music-making, however, continued to be the central activity of his life, and he became a member of the choirs of both New College and Christ Church Cathedral. The brilliant countertenor James Bowman was also a member of both choirs, and one of the sights in Oxford that year was the pair of them belting down the High

Street in a desperate bid to follow one evensong engagement with the next. The sequel to such frenzied activity was usually a less-than-sacred hour (or three) at the King's Arms—in order, you understand, to keep parched larynxes in peak form for the morrow.

One of Brian's most traumatic musical experiences occurred during his teaching-practice term that year. Graham Smallbone, director of music at Marlborough College, had asked him to sing the bass solos in Michael Tippett's *A Child of Our Time*. Brian treated the challenge a little too lightly, did little work on the piece, and bluffed his way through the rehearsal: it was, after all, 'only' a school performance. The entire com-

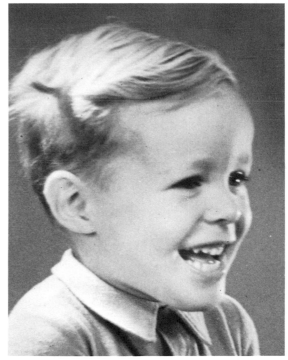

Nobody knows where the golden locks came from, but everybody knows where they went.

plexion of the occasion changed abruptly for Brian when, a couple of minutes before the performance began, Tippett himself was seen to be taking his seat in the audience.

Brian moved to London in September 1967 and joined the choir of Westminster Abbey—a post he continued to hold until the King's Singers became fully professional in 1971. During this period, apart from his work with the group, he sang with many ensembles, notably the John Aldiss Choir and Octet, the Louis Halsey Singers, the New English Singers (with whom he enjoyed a long-running Steve Race television series),

the Cantores in Ecclesia, the John Hoban Singers and, on occasions, the BBC Singers. He also toured as a member of a quintet (his sister Heather and Alastair Thompson were also members) in a show written by and starring Donald Swann—an experience that taught him much about theatre technique.

Brian is instantly recognisable as the one with the brow as extensive as it is noble. A non-smoker, he admits to pathetically few vices. He drank his first pint of beer at the age of four (the glass was earmarked for a front-row forward at his father's rugby club)

The organist entertains – not the Granada, Tooting, but the console at King's College Chapel.

154

and his second at the age of nineteen at the Eagle in Cambridge. In the years since then he has researched the subject thoroughly (except when working) and believes he is getting the hang of it. Since leaving London to live in the Cotswolds he has developed a passion for gardening and has discovered that he has green fingers. What little spare time he has he devotes to his two children, to tending the brassicas, and to beseeching the landlord of his favourite pub to open on Mondays.

With Sally and children Charlotte and Jonathan and a two-month-old sabbatical beard.

Alastair Thompson

Alastair, Bill Ives's predecessor as tenor in the group, was born in Dorset, the son of a schoolmaster who was an enthusiastic amateur singer. He began his musical life at the age of six, when he took piano lessons. The following year he applied for entry to the Westminster Abbey Choir School (which then had an annual intake of just five pupils); he failed that year but succeeded the next, and entered the school in 1954. At that time, he recalls, he was keen on both singing and sport; and while, owing to the exceptionally high standard of musical talent, he was not an outstanding singer at the school, his prowess on the sporting field singled him out.

More or less the opposite applied when he went to Lancing College on the Sussex downs, in 1958. Nonetheless, Lancing has a stronger musical tradition than many other public schools, and for Alastair it was always a pleasure to sing in the immense chapel there. At Lancing he gave up the piano and turned instead to the bassoon, soon becoming a member of the school orchestra. The need to wear spectacles discouraged his interest in sport—although later, playing for a rather ramshackle old boys' soccer team, he claims to have formed a ruthless full-back partnership with his Lancing contemporary, Tim Rice.

Curiously enough, throughout most of his years at Lancing, Alastair sang alto in the school choir, although he sometimes resorted to tenor when performing with the informal madrigal groups that were also very much part of the musical scene. In 1962 he went for the choral scholar trial at King's College, offering himself as either an alto or a tenor; he was offered a place as tenor in 1964. At this same trial was Neil Jenkins, who had been at Westminster Abbey Choir School with Alastair, and was to appear as a member of the Six in the formative year 1965-6 and the first concert at Hale Park; Neil went up to King's in 1963, and was thus an exact contemporary of Brian's. With a year to spare before going up to Cambridge, Alastair went to India on Voluntary Service Overseas and taught English at a school in the hill country near Poona.

Alastair's period at King's (1964-6) makes him the sole link with all the other King's scholars who formed the original group—Simon and Al (who left in 1965, Brian (who left in 1966), and Nigel (who arrived in 1966); and he had also performed with Tony as a member of the Tudor

A hang-over from the early days.

Singers. Like the first three, he was much involved with spare-time group singing at Cambridge, although then and later his interest lay primarily at the classical end of the repertoire. He especially remembers the coaching he, like most other choral scholars of his day, received from the distinguished singer and teacher John Carol Case, himself an old Kingsman.

Alastair's first concert for what was to become the King's Singers was at the Guildhall in York in 1965. He was on the recording, *Songs of Love*, in 1966, and took part in the second Hale Park concert in 1967, after completing a year at Oxford for his Diploma in Education. During the period between then and 1971, apart from appearing regularly with the group and with many of the professional choirs in London, he did an increasing amount of solo work, especially in oratorios.

His last appearance with the King's Singers was at the tenth anniversary concert in May 1978. By then he had set his heart on a solo career, and it might have been too late to fulfil this ambition if he had delayed the decision much longer. Since then he has spent more than a year in Germany, learning the language, extending his repertoire of *lieder*, and receiving further coaching in tenor singing. Now based in Paris, he is an established recital and oratorio soloist, and he is pondering the possibilities of opera.

Jeremy Jackman
Countertenor

Gemma Levine

Jeremy was born in 1952 and, shortly after disposing of his last nappy, found himself singing in the choir of St. Andrew's, Kingsbury. By the time he was eight years old, he had gone to St. Paul's Cathedral School, where he was a chorister, his name having been put forward by his organist at St. Andrew's, Barry Rose, who was later to become Director of Music at St. Paul's. Perhaps sensing that one day he would become involved with a load of ex-Oxbridge layabouts, he made a conscious decision (his own words) not to go to Cambridge, and studied for a music degree at the University of Hull. He then found himself in the difficult situation known to so many singers, of having a steady teaching job, in Morley, near Leeds, and at the same time singing with, for example, the BBC Northern Singers. Anyone who has been through that routine knows that teaching all day and singing all night is very exhausting—particularly if recently married, as was the case with Jeremy. So a decision had to be made and the world lost another dedicated member of the teaching profession. After moving south and studying with Paul Esswood (who, incidentally, had been a colleague of Brian Kay's in the choir of Westminster Abbey) he musically put himself about—singing with and for everybody and following a pattern established by so many others including other King's Singers. In March 1979 he joined the choir of Westminster Cathedral, just a year before accepting the offer of the King's Singers to join them.

His life must now follow the same pattern as theirs, but if he finds any problems along the way, he can always talk to Bill, who so quickly overcame them all! When he is not being a King's Singer, he lists his hobbies (in this order) as beer-making, beer-drinking, walking and cycling—this last being, he feels, a necessity, if only to work off the home-brewed, home-drunk beer!

Summer 1954.

158

Discography

A FRENCH COLLECTION: music by Jannequin, Jacotin, Passereau Certon, Willaert, Mornable, Poulenc etc.   *EMI CSD 3740*

THE KING'S SINGERS MADRIGAL COLLECTION: madrigals by Morley, Weelkes, Wilbye, Farmer, Lassus, Gastoldi etc.   *EMI CSD 3756*

CONCERT COLLECTION: including Henry VIII's *Pastime with Good Company*; Clement's *La Belle Marguerite* and songs by Grieg, Ridout, Josquin des Prés etc.   *EMI CSD 3766*

TALLIS: *The Lamentations of Jeremiah*
BYRD: motets – *Gaudeamus Omnes*; *Ne Irascaris, Domine*; *Domine, Salva Nos*; *Haec Dies*; *Vide, Domine*; *Ave Verum Corpus*   *EMI CSD 3779*

OUT OF THE BLUE: *Girl Talk*; *Dayton Ohio –1903*; *The Ash Grove*; *Lass of Richmond Hill*; *With You on my Mind*; *Wish You were Here* etc.   *EMI EMC 3023*

LOLLIPOPS: *I'm a Train*; *After the Gold Rush*; *Ma Belle Marguerite*; *Phil the Fluter's Ball*; *Widdecombe Fair* etc.   *EMI EMC 3093*

THE KING'S SINGERS SWING: *It Don't Mean a Thing*; *Blue Skies*; *Your Feet's Too Big*; *Basin Street Blues* etc.   *EMI EMC 3157*

CONTEMPORARY COLLECTION: music by Williamson, Dickinson, Penderecki, Patterson and Richard Rodney Bennett   *EMI EMD 5521*

THE KING'S SINGERS: *She's Leaving Home*; *The Windmills of your Mind*; *I Love You, Samantha*; *Morning has Broken*; *Après un rêve* etc.   *EMI OU 2118*

DECK THE HALL: songs for Christmas including *The Crown of Roses* (Tchaikovsky); *Mary had a Baby* (negro spiritual); *Hodie Christus Natus Est* (Byrd) etc.   *EMI HQS 1308*

THE KING'S SINGERS SING FLANDERS AND SWANN AND NOËL COWARD: including *A Transport of Delight*; *Misalliance*; *The Slow Train*; *Mad Dogs and Englishmen* etc.   *EMI EMC 3196*

10TH ANNIVERSARY CONCERT RECORD I
10TH ANNIVERSARY CONCERT RECORD II
Recorded live at the Royal Festival Hall

Record I includes songs of the Renaissance; Poulenc's *Quatres Petites Prières de Saint Francois d'Assise*   *EMI KS 1001*
Record II includes *Ten Years On*; *The Oak and the Ash*; *Widdecombe Fair*   *EMI KS 1002*

CONTINENTAL COLLECTION: German and Spanish part-songs by Hassler, Senfl, Lassus, Juan del Encina, Juan Vasquez and others   *EMI ASD 3557*

TEMPUS FUGIT: *Strawberry Fields Forever*; *Monday Monday*; *Space Oddity*; *Mr Tambourine Man* etc.   *EMI EMC 3268*

THE KING'S SINGERS SING 15 POPULAR GERMAN FOLK SONGS: *Ein Jäger Längs dem Weiher Ging*; *Die Forelle D.550* (Schubert) etc.   *EMI SCX 6609*

ATLANTIC BRIDGE: *Swing Low, Sweet Chariot*; *Dry Bones*; *Shenandoah*; *Beautiful Dreamer*; *Danny Boy* etc.   *EMI SCX 6615*

NEW DAY: *Nouveau Poor*; *Here Comes the Sun*; *Money, Money, Money*; *The Rhythm of Life* etc.   *EMI SCX 6629*

VICTORIAN COLLECTION: *Jenks's Vegetable Compound; Breathe Soft Ye Winds; The Long Day Closes* etc.   EMI ASD 3865

ENCORE: *The Peanut Vendor; Blow Away the Morning Dew; Summertime; Scarborough Fair* etc.   *Polydor* 2383320

CAPTAIN NOAH AND HIS FLOATING ZOO and HOLY MOSES   *Argo* ZBA 149

SCOTTISH MUSIC OF THE LATER MIDDLE AGES: *Trip and Go Hey; My Heartly Service; All Sons of Adam* etc.   *Scottish Records* SRSS 1

TAVENER: Requiem for Father Malachy
RCA LRL 15104

Gemma Levine